Robert Hudson

Songs of peace, love and joy

For Sabbath schools and gospel meetings

Robert Hudson

Songs of peace, love and joy
For Sabbath schools and gospel meetings

ISBN/EAN: 9783337223496

Printed in Europe, USA, Canada, Australia, Japan

Cover: Foto ©Thomas Meinert / pixelio.de

More available books at **www.hansebooks.com**

SONGS

OF

PEACE, LOVE,

AND

JOY,

BY

R. E. HUDSON,

FOR

Sabbath Schools and Gospel Meetings.

Published by

R. E. HUDSON, ALLIANCE, OHIO.

Single Copy,	–	–	–	–	–	.35
Per dozen,	–	–	–	–	–	$3.60
Per hundred,	–	–	–	–	–	25.00

2. BLESS THE LORD.

A SERVICE OF PRAISE.

Words and Music by R. E. HUDSON.

1. Bless the Lord,   Bless the Lord,   Bless the Lord, Bless the Lord, Amen.
2. For His peace,   For His peace,   Bless the Lord, Bless the Lord, Amen.
3. For His love,   For His love,   Bless the Lord, Bless the Lord, Amen.
4. For His joy,   For His joy,   Bless the Lord, Bless the Lord, Amen.

PRAYER.

Sing No. 150.—Songs of Peace, Love and Joy.

Pastor.—Great peace have they that love Thy law and nothing shall offend them."—Psalms 119: 165.

Congregation.—Thou wilt keep him in perfect peace, whose mind is stayed on Thee: because he trusteth in thee.—Isaiah 26: 3.

Pastor.—O that thou hadst hearkened to my commandments! then had thy peace been as a river, and thy righteousness as the waves of the sea.—Isaiah 48: 18.

Congregation.—Peace I leave with you, my peace I give unto you; not as the world giveth, give I unto you. Let not your heart be troubled, neither let it be afraid.—John 14: 27.

Sing No. 62.—Songs of Peace, Love and Joy.

Pastor.—Behold, what manner of love the Father hath bestowed upon us, that we should be called the sons of God: therefore the world knoweth us not, because it knew him not.—1 John 3: 1.

Congregation.—Hereby perceive we the love of God, because he laid down his life for us: and we ought to lay down our lives for the brethren. —1 John 3: 16.

Pastor.—And we have known and believed the love that God hath to us. God is love: and he that dwelleth in love dwelleth in God, and God in him. —1 John 4: 16.

Congregation.—There is no fear in love; but perfect love casteth out fear: because fear hath torment. He that feareth is not made perfect in love.--1 John 1: 18.

Sing No. 50.—Songs of Peace, Love and Joy.

Pastor.—Rejoice in the Lord alway; and again I say, rejoice.—Phil. 4: 4.

Congregation.—Rejoice evermore. Pray without ceasing. In everything give thanks; for this is the will of God in Christ Jesus concerning you.—1 Thess. 5: 16, 17, 18.

Pastor.—I will bless the Lord at all times: His praise shall continually be in my mouth.—Ps. 34: 1.

Congregation.—Glory ye in his holy name: let the heart of them rejoice that seek the Lord.—Ps. 105: 3.

Sing No. 93.—Songs of Peace, Love and Joy.
Sing No. 120.—Songs of Peace, Love and Joy.
Sing No. 128.—Songs of Peace, Love and Joy.
Sing No. 79.—Songs of Peace, Love and Joy.

DESERT.

1. Oh, for a thou - sand tongues. to sing My great Re-deem-er's praise:
2. My gra-cious Mas - ter and my God, As-sist me to pro-claim,
3. Je - sus! the name that charms our fears, That bids our sor - rows cease;
4. He breaks the power of can - celled sin, He sets the prisoner free.

My great Re-deem-er's praise; The glo-ries of my God and King,
As-sist me to pro-claim, To spread through all the earth a - broad,
That bids our sor-rows cease; Tis mu - sic in the sin - ner's ears,
He sets the prisoner free. His blood can make the foul - est clean;

The tri-umphs of his grace, The triumphs of his
The hon - ors of thy name, The hon - ors of thy
'Tis life, and health, and peace, 'Tis life, and health, and
His blood a-vailed for me, His blood a-vailed for

The tri-umphs of his grace,
The hon-ors of thy name,
'Tis life, and health, and peace,
His blood a-vailed for me.

The tri-umphs of his grace,
The hon - ors of thy name,
'Tis life, and health, and peace,
His blood a-vailed for me,

grace, The tri - umphs of his grace.
name, The hon - ors of thy name.
peace, 'Tis life, and health, and peace.
me, His blood a - vailed for me.

4. # WHEN WE ARRIVE AT HOME.

Words and Music by R. E. Hudson.

1. There's a crown for ev'-ry head, And there's joy for ev'-ry heart,
2. There's a joy in trust-ing here, And there's love with-out a fear,
3. Oh, come and join our band, For right and truth we'll stand,

CHORUS.

At the end of our jour - ney, We'll re-ceive a crown,

Joy for ev' - ry heart, joy for ev' - ry heart, Who will
Love with - out a fear, love with - out a fear; Re-joic-
Right and truth we'll stand, right and truth we'll stand Till right

We'll re - ceive a crown, we'll re - ceive a crown At the

in His vine - yard en - ter, And brave - ly do
ing ev - er - more Un - til the con-
shall con - quer wrong; Then we'll join the

end of our jour - ney We'll re - ceive

his part Till we ar - rive at home?
flict's o'er. And we ar - rive at home.
washed throng, When we ar - rive at home.

a crown, When we ar - rive at home.

RESTING.

Respectfully dedicated to my esteemed friends, Rev. C. G. Hudson and wife.

R. E. HUDSON.

1. Resting on the faithfulness of Christ our Lord; Resting on the fulness of His
2. Resting His guiding hand for un- days; Resting His shadow from the
   'neath   tracked   'neath
3. Resting in the fortress while the foe is nigh; Resting in the lifeboat while the
4. Resting and believing, let us onward press, Resting in Himself, the Lord, our

own sure word; Rest-ing on His pow-er, on His love un-told;
noon-tide rays; Rest-ing at the ev-en-tide be-neath His wing,
waves roll high; Rest-ing in His char-iot for the swift glad race;
Right-eous-ness; Rest-ing and re-joic-ing, let His saved ones sing,

Rest-ing on his covenant secured of old.
In the fair pavilion of our Saviour King.
Resting, always resting in His boundless grace.
Glory, glory, glory be to Christ our King.

Rest - ing on His promise sweet,

Resting, every moment resting

Rest - ing, sitting at His feet, Glad - ly

Resting, every moment resting,

Waiting, ever ready waiting

at His call I'll go, Trusting in His blood that cleanseth white as snow.

6. I'VE WASHED MY ROBES.

E. O. E.   E. O. Excell.

1. My robes were once all stain'd with sin, I knew not how to make them clean;
2. That prom-ise, "who-so-ev-er will," In-clud-ed me,—includes me still;
3. I do not doubt, nor do I say, "I hope the stains are wash'd away,"
4. Oh, who will come and wash to-day, 'Till all their stains are wash'd away;

Un-til a voice said, sweet and low, "Go wash, I'll make them white as snow."
I came and ev-er since, I know, His blood, it cleanseth white as snow.
For in his Word I read it so: His blood, it cleanseth white as snow.
Un-til by faith they see and know Their robes are wash'd as white as snow?

CHORUS.

I've wash'd my robes........... in Je-sus' blood............ And he has
I've wash'd my robes   in Jesus' blood,

made......them white as snow........I've wash'd my robes... in Je-sus'
And he has made   them white as snow,   I've wash'd my robes

blood......... And he has made.........them white as snow.
in Jesus' blood,   And he has made them white as snow, white as snow.

By per. J. H. S.

1. When I sur-vey the wondrous cross On which the Prince of glo-ry
2. For-bid it, Lord, that I should boast, Save in the death of Christ, my
3. See, from his head, his hands, his feet, Sor-row and love flow mingled
4. Were the whole realm of nature mine, That were a pres-ent far too

died, My rich-est gain, I count but loss, And pour contempt on all my pride.
God; All the vain things that charm me most, I sac-ri-fice them to his blood.
down: Did e'er such love and sorrow meet, Or thorns compose so rich a crown?
small; Love so a-maz-ing, so di-vine, Demands my soul, my life, my all.

CHORUS.

He ransomed me, He ransomed me, My Sav-iour died to ran-som me,

He ransomed me, He ransomed me, With his own blood He ransomed me.

Copyrighted, 1884, by R. E. HUDSON.

8. THE HARVEST IS PASSING.

Words and Music by R. E. HUDSON.

Slow.

1. The harvest is passing of blessings so free, The harvest is passing, He
2. The harvest is passing, al-rea-dy the fields Are whit'ning for harvest, but
3. The harvest is passing, no seed have I sown, No grain have I gathered, no
4. The harvest is passing, Oh, hasten to-day, The summer will end soon, Oh

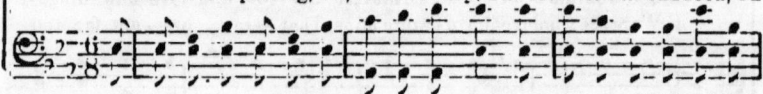

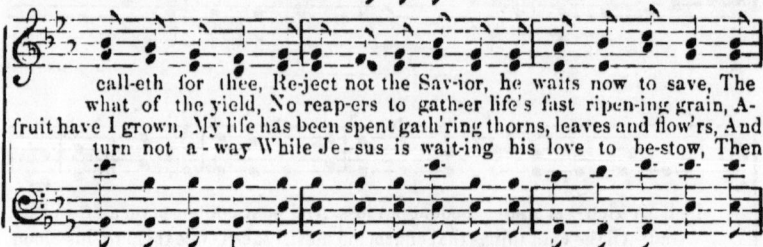

call-eth for thee, Re-ject not the Sav-ior, he waits now to save, The
what of the yield, No reap-ers to gath-er life's fast ripen-ing grain, A-
fruit have I grown, My life has been spent gath'ring thorns, leaves and flow'rs, And
turn not a-way While Je-sus is wait-ing his love to be-stow, Then

CHORUS. The har......

Lord of the harvest his life free-ly gave.)
las, when he calleth, he call-eth in vain. |
I'm not pre-pared for those heav'nly bowers. } The harvest is passing, The
forth to his ser-vice, say glad-ly I'll go.)

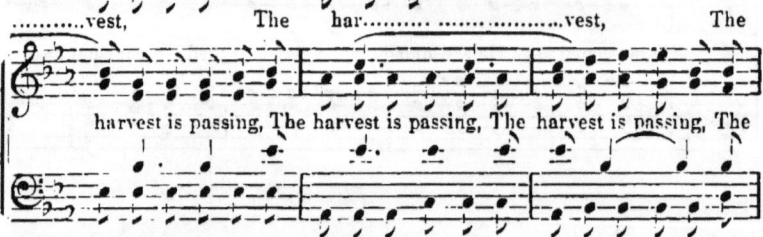

...........vest, The har......... ....vest, The

harvest is passing, The harvest is passing, The harvest is passing, The

sum......... ....mer

summer is end-ed, The summer is ended, And I am not saved.

TOUCH NOT! TASTE NOT! HANDLE NOT! 9.

J. B. TAYLOR.

TOM C. NEAL.

1. The gob-let is sparkling and tempting to view, Yet
2. The tempter exclaims "there's a balm in its ware That will
3. Let not friendship too press-ing-ly urge thee to dare, With the

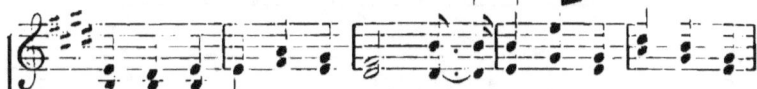

why should I per-il my soul? The juice of the grape may be
free thee from sor-row and care; But a ser-pent sits coil-ing him-
temp-ter to tri-fle and toy, Lest the de-mon Intemp'rance bring

lus-cious when new, Yet a de-mon still lurks in the bowl!
self on the brim; Of his sting I would warn ye, be-ware!
sor-row and care, And too dear-ly you pay for your joy!

CHORUS.
ff

Oh, touch not! taste not! Handle not the ruby wine, ruby wine!

Oh, touch not the cup, Taste not the cup!

Oh, touch not! taste not! Handle not the ru-by wine!

Oh, touch not the cup! Taste not the cup!

10.

I WILL FOLLOW JESUS.

Respectfully dedicated to Mrs. Amanda Blackburn.

R. E. Hudson.

1. Down in the valley with my Saviour I would go, Where the flow'rs are bloom-
2. Down in the valley with my Saviour I would go, Where the storms are sweep-
3. Down in the valley, or up-on the mountain steep, Close be-side my Sav-

ing and the sweet wa-ters flow; Ev'-ry-where He leads me I would
ing, and the dark wa-ters flow; With His hand to lead me, I will
iour would my soul ev-er keep; He will lead me safe-ly in the

fol-low, fol-low on, Walk-ing in His foot-steps till the crown be won.
ev-er, nev-er fear; Dangers can-not fright me, if my Lord is near.
path that He has trod, Up to where they gath-er on the hills of God.

CHORUS.

Fol-low, fol-low, I will fol-low Je-sus! Any-where, ev'-ry-where,

I will fol-low on; Fol-low, fol-low, I will fol-low

I WILL FOLLOW JESUS.—Concluded.

Je - sus! Ev' - ry-where He leads me I will fol - low on. .

THERE IS ROOM.

Abbie Mills.
Duet.

G. W. Fields. 11.

1. There is room for you, my brother, In the straight and narrow way;
2. There is room for you, my sis-ter, In the home where Je-sus dwells;
3. There is room for you, be-liev-er, In the high - way of the Lord;

If all filth - i - ness of spir-it And of flesh you cast a - way;
Rise ar-rayed in His own beauty, And sit down by liv - ing wells;
Yes, there's room for who-so-ev-er Will o - bey His writ -ten word:

Oh! the things to which you're clinging Ne'er can sat-is - fy the soul:
Golden wealth and glittering treasure Ne'er can give that peace within,
Do not, then, despise your birthright, And a mess of pottage choose;

Clouds of wit - ness - es are singing; Je-sus' blood a -lone makes whole.
But there's blessings without measure, When thy heart is free from sin.
Do not shut your eyes 'mid sunlight, And the path in darkness lose.

CHORUS.

There is room, There is room In the straight and narrow way;

Will you come, Will you come, Will you come, His call o - bey?

12. SING OF HIS LOVE.

Words and Music by R. E. Hudson.

Praise the Lord, Praise the Lord, Praise the Lord
Praise the Lord, Praise the Lord, Praise the Lord,

(Omit 2d ending only.)

Ritard. *Fine.*

for-ev-er-more, for-ev - er - more! Oh, worship the Lord in the

beau-ty of ho - li-ness, Sing un-to Him, and tell of His love.

Sing of His love to me, Sing how He free - ly

gave His life for thee, Sing through His blood we may from sin be free,

Ritard. | *Solo first time.*

Sing of His love. For God so loved the world

For God so loved the world

that He gave His on - ly Son, His

that He gave, He gave His Son,

on - ly be - got - ten Son, That who - so - ev - er be -

liev - eth in Him, That who - so - ev - er be - liev-eth in Him,

D.C.

Should not per - ish, but have ev - er - last - ing life.

14. THE WANDERING STRANGER.

1. "Say, whith-er, wander-ing stranger, Ah, with - er dost thou roam?
2. "But want, and woe have driv-en, The ro - ses from thy cheek,
3. "Come then, be - nign in - quir - er, And join me on my way;

O'er this wide world a ran - ger, Hast thou no friend, no home?'"
And gar-ments rent and riv - en, Thy pov - er - ty be - speak,"
I'm jour-neying to a coun-try, Where beams an end - less day,

"Yes, I've a friend who nev - er Is ab - sent from my side,
"The food with which the an - gels, Would all de - light - ed be,
Where saints and an - gels fall - ing, Be - fore the great white throne.

And I've a home where ev - er In peace I shall a - bide."
And robes of dazz - ling bright-ness Are now a - wai - ting me."
To you, to me are call - ing, Haste, pil-grim, hast - en home."

THE ALTERED MOTTO.

15.

Theo. Monod.
With expression.

Thos. O. Lowe.

1. Oh, the bit - ter pain and sor - row That a time could ev - er be,
2. Yet He found me; I be - held Him, Bleed-ing on th' accursed tree;
3. Day by day His ten - der mer - cy, Heal-ing, help-ing, full and free;
4. Higher than the high - est heav-ens, Deep-er than the deep-est sea,

When I proud-ly said to Je - sus, "All of self and none of Thee."
And my wist - ful heart said faint- ly, "Some of self and some of Thee."
Brought me lower, while I whis-pered, "Less of self and more of Thee."
Lord, Thy love at last has conquered, "None of self and all of Thee."

Rit.

All of self and none of Thee, All of self and none of Thee,
Some of self and some of Thee, Some of self and some of Thee,
Less of self and more of Thee, Less of self and more of Thee,
None of self and all of Thee, None of self and all of Thee,

Rit.

When I proud - ly said to Je - sus, "All of self and none of Thee."
And my wist - ful heart said faint-ly, "Some of self and some of Thee."
Brought me low - er, while I whispered, "Less of self and more of Thee."
Lord, Thy love at last has conquered, "None of self and all of Thee."

WHITER THAN THE SNOW.

Mrs. M. A. KIDDER.   J. A. DAILEY.

1. Fear not, little flock, says the Saviour divine, The Father has willed that the
2. Far whiter than snow, and as fair as the day,—For Christ is the fountain to
3. You sheep, that was lost in the valley of sin, Was found by the shepherd, who

kingdom be thine, O soil not your garments with sin here below,—My sheep and my
wash guilt away; Oh, give him, poor sinner, that burden of thine, And enter the
gathered him in; With songs of thanksgiving the hills did resound, My friends and my

CHORUS.

lambs must be whiter than snow.) Whit .... er than snow,
fold with the ninety-and-nine.   }
neighbors the lost sheep is found.) Whiter than the snow,   I long to be, dear Saviour,

Whit................. er than snow,   Whit................. er than
Whiter than the snow,   I long to be   Whiter than the snow,

Repeat Chorus pp.

snow,   Whit................. er than snow.
I long to be, dear Saviour, Whiter than the snow,   Whiter than the snow.

J. H.   Mrs. Jos. F. Knapp, by per.

1. Soldiers of th'eternal King, Speed the watchword, give it wing, Let it thro' the
2.   La - bel it on ev'ry door, Place it high the pulpit o'er, Let it stand for-
3. Place it on the chisel'd stone, Where the mourners weep alone; Grave it on the

churches ring, Up for Je - sus stand! Write it on the temple's spire,
ev - er - more! Up for Je - sus stand! Blazon it in mansion-halls,
monarch's throne, Up for Je - sus stand! Let the press, whose wheels of might

Ut-ter it with tongues of fire, Sire to son and son to sire, Up for Jesus stand!
Pencil it on prison walls; Do and dare as duty calls, Up for Jesus stand!
Roll for reason and for right, Flash it on the nation's sight; Up for Jesus stand!

CHORUS.

Sire to son and son to sire, Up for Je-sus stand! Up for Je-sus stand!
Do and dare as du-ty calls, Up for Je-sus stand!
Flash it on the nation's sight, Up for Je-sus stand!   Jesus stand!

Up for Jesus stand! Speed the watchword, give it wing, And up for Jesus stand!
Jesus stand,

GO FORTH, MEN OF GOD.

Respectfully dedicated to the North Indiana Conference, M. E. Church.

FIRM.

Words and Music by R. E. HUDSON.

1. Go forth, men of God, and stand for the right, Gird on the whole armor, and
2. Go forth, men of God, your captain leads on, Stand forth in the conflict till
3. Go forth, men of God, sal-va-tion pro-claim, Sal-va-tion from sin, its pol-

stand in his might, The world may op-pose, and sin may de-fy, Let
vic-t'ry is won, The joy of the Lord yours ev-er may be, Till
lu-tion and shame, His life as ran-som for sin-ners he gave, That

CHORUS. Go preach, Go

this be your watch-word: "We'll win though we die.
serv-ice is end-ed and you are set free.
he through his blood might abundantly save.

Go preach the word,

tell

Go tell the world sal-va-tion full and free, Fear not, the Gos-

pel's pow'r pro-claim, And shout the vic-to-ry.

Copyrighted, 1884, by R. E. Hudson.

I. B.　　　　　　　　　　　　　　　　By per. I. Baltzell.

1. Lo! our ves - sel's on the o-cean, See it glid - ing swiftly by,
2. Come on board the ves-sel, stranger, Sail with us o'er life's rough sea;
3. When we gain the port of glo - ry, When we reach our home above,

And a - mid the wild com-mo-tion, Hear the sail - ors loud-ly cry:
For we fear no want or dan - ger, From all per - ils we are free
We'll re-peat the old, old sto - ry, Of the Sav - iour's dying love.

CHORUS.

Stand the storm, Stand the storm, We will an - or by and by,

It won't be long, It won't be long, ‖:we will anchor,:‖ ‖: by and by.:‖

Stand the storm, Stand the storm, We will an - chor by and by, by and by.

It won't be long, It won't be long, we will anchor, we will anchor By and By, ·

20. SINCE I HAVE BEEN REDEEMED.

E. O. E.　　　　　　　　　　　　　　　　　　　　E. O. Excell.

1. I have a *song* I love to sing, Since I have been redeemed, Of
2. I have a *Christ* that sat-is-fies, Since I have been redeemed, To
3. I have a *Wit-ness*, bright and clear, Since I have been redeemed, Dis-
4. I have a *joy* I can't ex-press, Since I have been redeemed, All
5. I have a *home* pre-pared for me, Since I have been redeemed, Where

CHORUS.

my Re-deem-er, Saviour, King, Since I have been re-deemed. Since
do His will my high-est prize, Since I have been re-deemed.
pell-ing ev'-ry doubt and fear, Since I have been re-deemed.
through His blood and righteousness, Since I have been re-deemed.
I shall dwell e-ter-nal-ly, Since I have been re-deemed. Since

I............... have been re-deemed,
I have been redeemed, Since I have been redeemed, Since I have been

1st. | **2d.**

redeemed, I will glory in His name, I will glo-ry in my Saviour's name.

MY BOY IS COMING HOME TO-NIGHT. 21

Words and Music by R. E. Hudson.

1. I see a mother wait-ing, She's wait-ed wea-ry years, The
2. The boy she loves has wandered far Away from home and friends; But
3. O wandering boy, come home, They're waiting for you there; Oh,

boy she loved is far from home, Oh, see her bit-ter tears; But
now in want he thinks of one Whose heart in pi-ty bends. He
hear them sing the sweet old hymn, And kneel in evening pray'r. They

glad good news she soon will hear, 'Twill make her sad heart light, The
thinks of fa-ther's tender care, Of sis-ter's face so bright; And
wait, they long for thy re-turn From darkness un-to light; Let

CHORUS.

boy she loves, to her so dear, Is coming home to-night. Coming home to-night, He's
now with eager step he turns, He's coming home to-night.
angels sing, while hearts rejoice, He's coming home to-night.

coming home to-night, The boy she loves, to her so dear, Is coming home to-night.

Coming home to-night,

22. PRODIGAL CHILD, COME HOME.

Words and Music by R. E. HUDSON.

1. Prodigal child, come home, come home, Out in the desert so bleak and wild,
2. Prodigal child, come home, come home, Father has mansions prepared for thee,
3. Prodigal child, come home, come home, Why feed on husks when plenty's in store?

Stay not a-way, the night is dark, Fath-er is wait-ing to greet his child.
Turn from thy sins and let Him in, Je-sus has suffered, salvation is free.
Beau-ti-ful robe, and then a crown, One that en-du-reth for ev - er more.

CHORUS.

Come home, Prodigal child, come home, Never to wander more, never to roam,

Fath-er is wait-ing, Fath-er is wait-ing, Prodigal child, come ome, come home.

Copyrighted, 1884, by R. E. Hudson.

I COME JUST AS I AM.

Words and Music by R. E. HUDSON.

1. O Lord, thine on-ly will I be, And now I glad-ly come to thee,
2. My sins, like mountains round me rise, But thou hast made the sac-ri-fice;
3. I come to thee with sin oppressed, Thy prom-ise is I'll give thee rest;
4. For me, dear Saviour, thou hast died, Thy precious blood is now ap-plied,

I take thy prom-ise made to me, And come just as I am.
Now to my heart the blood ap-ply, I come just as I am,
In trust-ing thee I now am blest, I come just as I am.
Now in thy prom-ise I con-fide, And come just as I am.

Take me as I am,............... Take me as I am,
Take me as I am, Take me as I am, Take me as I am, Take me

as I am, Without one plea I come to thee, Oh, take me as I am.

Copyrighted, 1884, by R. E. Hudson.

TELL IT OUT!

FRANCES RIDLEY HAVERGAL.

1. Tell it out a-mong the hea-then, that the Lord is King!
2. Tell it out a-mong the na-tions, that the Sav-iour reigns!
3. Tell it out a-mong the hea-then, Je-sus reigns a-bove!

Tell it out! tell it out! that the Lord is King!
Tell it out! tell it out! that the Sav-iour reigns!
Tell it out! tell it out! Je-sus reigns a-bove!

Tell it out! Tell it out!
Tell it out! Tell............... it out!

Tell it out!................ Tell it out!

Tell it out a-mong the na-tions, bid them shout and sing!
Tell it out a-mong the hea-then, bid them burst their chains!
Tell it out a-mong the na-tions that his reign is love!

Tell it out! Tell it out! bid them shout and sing!
Tell it out! Tell it out! bid them burst their chains!
Tell it out! Tell it out! that his reign is love!

FINE.

Tell it out!................ Tell it out! Tell it out!
Tell it out! Tell it out! Tell it out!

Tell it out! Tell............... it out!

Tell it out................................

Tell it out with a - do - ra - tion that he shall in -crease;
Tell it out a - mong the weep - ing ones, that Je - sus lives;
Tell it out a - mong the high-ways and the lanes at home;

Tell it out.........../......................

That the might - y King of Glo - ry is the King of Peace.
Tell it out a - mong the wea - ry ones what rest he gives;
Let it ring a - cross the moun-tains and the o - cean's foam

Tell it out with . ju - bi - la - tion, tho' the waves may roar,
Tell it out a - mong the sin - ners, that he came to save;
Like the sound of ma - ny wa - ters let the glad shout be.

D. S. al fine.

That he sit - teth on the wa - ter floods our King for - ev - er - more!
Tell it out a - mong the dy-ing, that he tri-umphed o'er the grave!
Till it ech - o and re - ech - o from the is-lands to the sea!

WEARY ONE, REST.

R. E. HUDSON.

1. I heard the voice of Je-sus say: "Come un-to me and rest!
2. I came to Je-sus as I was, Wea-ry, and worn, and sad;
3. I heard the voice of Je-sus say: "Behold! I free-ly give
4. I came to Je-sus, and I drank Of that life-giv-ing stream;

CHORUS.

Lay down, poor weary one, Lay down your head upon my breast. Je-sus is
I found in Him a resting-place, And He has made me glad.
The living water—thirsty one, Stoop down, and drink, and live."
My thirst was quenched, my soul is saved, And now I live in Him.

waiting, Je-sus is waiting, Je-sus is wait-ing for you and me;

Je-sus is waiting, Je-sus is waiting, Je-sus is waiting for thee.

J. A. C.
Moderato. Thos. O. Lowe.

1. Re-deem-ing Love! Re-deem-ing Love! This is the
2. The an - gel hosts all wond'ring see, But fail to
3. And here on earth the pow'r is giv'n To sing this
4. Oh, shout a - loud, ye sons of men! Tell the glad

Rit.

theme of saints a - bove; Ar-ray'd in heaven's own spot-less
solve the mys - ter-y; They here, en-tranced, this no - ble
sweet - est song of heav'n; And our poor voi - ces e'en to
tid - ings o'er a - gain; Oh, earth be - low! oh, heav'n a-

Rit.

white, Chant they this song with pure de - light.
song, Of souls re - deemed—a might - y throng.
raise, In notes of loud and joy - ous praise.
bove, Sing ye the song, Re - deem - ing Love!

Refrain, slowly.
ff mf pp Rit.

Re-deem-ing Love! Re - deem-ing Love! Re - deem-ing Love!

28. OUR CHERISHED LOVED ONES.

DUET.   By per. WILL. C. BROWN.

1. In that bright and golden cit - y, Of the land far, far a - way,
2. In that land where all is sun - shine, And no clouds can in-ter-vene,
3. In that home of life and beau - ty, Is the dwelling place of God;

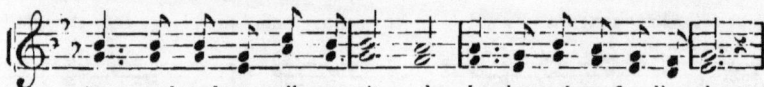

Are our loved ones all u - nit - ed, In the realms of endless day;
Where the brightest saints of heav - en Are be - hold-en in the scene;
And He gives to us the prom - ise, If we'll take Him for our guide;

There a - mid an - gel - ic se - raphs, Of the land be-yond the sky,
There they dwell with sweetest rap-ture, In the bliss that love be-stows;
That when here our days are end - ed, And we go a - cross the stream,

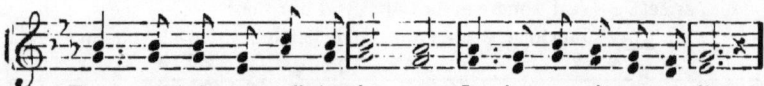

They may help to swell the cho - rus, In the songs that nev-er die.
And no mor - tal hand can rob them, Of the glo - ry of their souls.
He will lead us thro' the gate-way, To the home of the redeemed.

CHORUS.

We shall see our cherished loved ones In that land far, far a - way,

We shall see our cherished loved ones In that land far, far a-way,

In the cit - y bright and gold-en, In the realms of endless day.

In the cit - y bright and golden, In the realms of endless day.

WHAT DID JESUS SAY ?

R. E. HUDSON.

1. Je - sus in the tem - ple, with the doc - tors wise,

Asking wondrous questions, giving deep replies; When his parents found him,

seeking night and day, Found him in the tem - ple, what did Jesus say?
[LUKE ii : 49.]

CHORUS. (For last verse.)

Come, ye blessed of my Fath-er, In-her - it the kingdom prepared for you,

From the foundation of the world, From the foundation of the world. A-men.

2. At the well of Jacob, resting by its brink,
Bidding the Samaritan give to him to drink,
When she asked of Jesus where men ought to pray,
At the well of Jacob, what did Jesus say?
[JOHN iv : 21, 23.]

3. On the sea of Galilee, when the storm was high,
Save us, Lord! we perish! his disciples cry;
While they marvel greatly, as the winds obey,
On the sea of Galilee, what did Jesus say?
[MATT. viii : 26.]

4. Coming into Bethany, meeting, full of gloom,
Martha, mourning Lazarus, lying in the tomb—
Of the Resurrection, and the last Great Day,
Coming into Bethany, what did Jesus say?
[JOHN xi : 23. 25.]

5. Weeping o'er Jerusalem, city of the King,
Whom he would have gathered 'neath his loving wing,
Mourning for her children, going far astray,
Weeping o'er Jerusalem, what did Jesus say?
[MATT. xxiii : 37.

6. From that cross of sorrow, ere his soul went up,
As he drank the fullness of the bitter cup,
Looking on his enemies, in their dark array,
From that cross of sorrow, what did Jesus say?
[LUKE xxiii : 34.]

7. On the hills of heaven, in the world above,
Where his faithful children share his wondrous love,
All their sins forgiven, in that blessed day,
On the hills of heaven, what will Jesus say?
[MATT. xxv. 34.]

30. TREASURES OF HEAVEN.

By per. T. C. O'KANE.

1. There's a crown in heaven for the striving soul, Which the blessed Je-
2. There's a Rest in heaven for the weary soul, 'Tis for all by care
3. There's a home in heaven for the faithful soul, In the many man-

sus himself will place On the head of each who shall faithful prove
and by sin oppressed; To the sons of God it remaineth sure,
sions prepared above, Where the glorified shall forever sing,

Even unto death in the heavenly race, Oh, may that crown in heaven be
And the Prophet says, 'tis a "glorious rest," Oh, may that Rest in heaven be
Of a Saviour's free and unbounded love, Oh, may that Home in heaven be

Oh, may that crown

mine, And I among the angels shine; Be thou, O

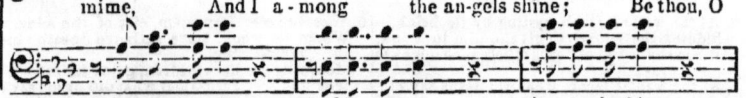

in heaven be mine, And I among the angels shine;

Lord! my daily guide, Let me ever in thy love abide.

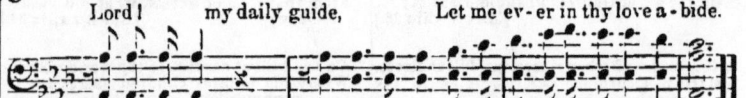

Be thou, oh Lord! my daily guide, Let me ever in thy love abide.

Rev. H. B. Hartzler. J. H. T., by per.

1. There is joy in heaven, where the angels dwell, And the gladsome notes of rejoicing swell.
2. There is joy in heaven, when the lost is found, And the golden streets with the news resound,
3. There is joy in heaven, that begins below, Where the tears of grief and repentance flow ;

When the tidings come from the world below, That a soul is saved from eternal woe.
Till the tide of song like an ocean rolls Unto Him who died for the love of souls.
And the saints of God with the angels share In the praise that rings like an anthem there.

Chorus.

Beautiful song ! Beautiful song ! Beautiful song ! Beautiful song of
Beautiful song ! Beautiful song ! Beautiful song ! Beautiful

mp *cresc.*

joy ! Ev'-ry harp is at-tuned un - to the sound, And the angels re-
song of joy !

joice that the lost is found, Beautiful song ! Beautiful song of joy !

Song of joy, Beau-ti-ful song, hap-py song of joy !

32.   MY ANGEL MOTHER.

Words and Music by R. E. Hudson.

Inst.

1. Last night there came a let - ter,   'Twas from my sis - ter dear;
2. She told me they were wait-ing,   Till I came home once more,
3. She soon shall see her dar-ling,   I start for home to - day
4. Just now there comes a mes-sage,   They laid her 'neath the sod,

She told me of my moth-er,   Her love, her pray'rs, her tears.
For soon my dar-ling moth-er,   Must cross that oth - er shore.
Once more to see my moth-er,   And sis - ters far a - way.
But oh! her an - gel spir - it   Is dwel-ling now with God.

CHORUS.

Then blame me not for weep-ing,   Oh, blame me not, I pray,
CHORUS for last verse only.
Then blame me not for weep-ing,   Oh, blame me not, I pray,

For I have an an - gel moth-er   In the old home far a - way.
For I have an an - gel moth-er   In that bright land far a - way.

PRAYER FOR GUIDANCE. 33.

Words by R. E. H.　　　　　　　　　　　　　ARRANGED.

1. Je - sus, tend-er shep-herd, hear me In the morn-ing fresh and bright;
2. Let my tongue be kept from speaking Words of envy, wrath, or guile;
3. Let my feet be kept from straying In - to sin of an - y kind;

Let Thy Spi-rit dwell with - in me, Keep me walk-ing in the light.
Let my heart be kept from feel-ing Aught but what becomes Thy child.
Lead me not in - to temp-ta - tion, All this day, Lord, keep me thine.

S: CHORUS.

Keep me walk - ing in the light, Keep me walk - ing in the

walk-ing, beautiful light, walk-ing,

light,......... Keep me walk - - ing in the light,.........

beautiful light, walking, beautiful light,
Repeat softly :S:

Keep me walk-ing in the beau-ti-ful light of God.

light of God.

34. WE MEAN THIS WORLD FOR GOD.

Arr. by R E. H.

1. We mean this world for God, We can-not be de-nied; For
2. Je - sus, the Lord of Hosts, Shall lead the Ar - my on, For
3. Oh, for more sold-iers bold, Who for our God will fight Like

for God, denied,

He has bought it by His blood, For this our Sav-iour died.
God, the Son, and Ho - ly Ghost, With Him hath made us one.
those dear men who fought of old, And served with such de - light.

We mean to spread His grace Where so much sin a - bounds, Thro'
Wield-ing the Spi - rit's sword, Which pier-ces hearts of steel, Which
Oh, for more men of power, Who naught on earth can scare, Who

His grace, abounds,

ev - ery clime, in ev - ery place, Sal - va - tion songs to sound......
might - y power we'll speak the word, And make the re - bels kneel......
al - ways in the dark-est hour For God will do and dare......

CHORUS.

This world shall be set free, This is our rallying cry. From

Copyrighted, by R. E. Hudson, 1884. set free,

WE MEAN THIS WORLD.—Concluded.

land to land, from sea to sea Our col - ors we will fly,

Ad - vance, ad - vance, The bu - gle sounds ad - vance, Ad-

ad-vance, ad-vance,

vance, ad - vance, The bu - gle sounds ad - vance.

ad-vance, ad-vance,

LORD, ABIDE WITH ME. 35.

Words by a BLIND POETESS.

1. Je - sus, Sav-iour! hear my call, Sin - ful though my heart may be;
2. Thou hast died the lost to save, Died to set the cap - tive free;
3. Fill me with thy love di-vine, Con - se - crate my life to thee;

Thou, my life, my hope, my all, Lord, a - bide with me.
Thou didst tri - umph o'er the grave, Lord, a - bide with me.
Bend my stub - born will to thine, Lord, a - bide with me.

36. WILL IT PAY?

By per. J. W. BUGGLES.

1. There's a question that comes to us, And it comes many times in a day;
2. If a com-rade in-vite you to drink, Or en-gage for some wa-ger to play,
3. Or perhaps you are led to pro-fane The name of the Lord ev-'ry day,
4. Oh, con-sid-er the words of the Lord, For they teach us a far bet-ter way;

Oh, it comes as a kind an-gel's call, That says, "Count the cost—
I be-seech you, my friend, stop and think, Con-sid-er the cost—
Oh, how oft take his dear name in vain! What think you, my boy—
And his coun-sels true pleas-ure af-ford, In them we can trust—

will it pay?" Will it pay in the con-flict of sin, If we bar-ter our
will it pay? Will it pay to lose Heaven for a cup That will on-ly bring
will it pay? Will it pay you to for-feit your right To the beau-ti-ful
it will pay? When this brief life of conflict is o'er, Oh, how blest if we

day of e-ter-ni-ty is near, *Oh,*
soul-life a-way? Tho' the pleas-ures of time we may win, Do you
grief and dis-may? "Oh, then, why will ye die?" give it up; Oh, break
man-sions a-bove? To be ban-ished for-ev-er in night, Far a-
hear Je-sus say, "Come, ye faith-ful, and rest ev-er-more." Surely
stand be-fore the great white throne, *Oh,*

WILL IT PAY?—Concluded.

then do you think it will pay?
think, af-ter all, it will pay?
off from its chains while ye may.
way from God's boun-ti-ful love?
this will be joy; This will pay.
then we will find it will pay.

Will it pay, Will it pay, Will it

AFTER LAST VERSE:

It will pay, It will pay, It will

Will it pay,

pay,
pay.

Thus to tri-fle this brief life a-way?
It will pay on the great judgment day,

D. C. :8:

When the
When we

Will it pay,

Will it pay,

I'LL BE THERE.   37.

ARRANGED.

1 { Je - sus, my all, to heav'n is gone, }
  { He whom I fix my hopes up-on; } When the last trumpet sounds, I'll be there.

2 { His track I see and I'll pur-sue, }
  { The narrow way, till Him I view, } When the last trumpet sounds, I'll be there.

3 { Then will I tell to sinners round, }
  { What a dear Saviour I have found } When the last trumpet sounds, I'll be there.

CHORUS.   *Repeat ff*

I'll be there,   I'll be there! When the last trumpet sounds, I'll be there.
  I'll be there,   I'll be there,

38. GOD IS COMING.

MRS. SUE. M. O. HOFFMAN, by per

1. God is coming! God is coming! shout aloud the glad re-frain;
2. God is coming! God is coming! roll the notes of joy on high;
3. God is coming! God is coming! and the hosts of sin are strong;
4. God is coming! God is coming! O lift up your hearts and pray!

Send the cry from town and cit-y to the vil-lage, ham-let, plain;
Ev-ery blood-bought son of Je-sus, ral-ly to your lead-er's cry!
We will meet them bravely, bold-ly, and the fight will not be long.
In the fight 'twixt light and darkness he will need strong arms to-day.

D.S. Every man be up on du-ty, For Je-hov-ah comes this way.

God is com-ing! hear the an-gels shout the tidings from above;
God is com-ing! God is com-ing! rub your rus-ty ar-mor bright,
God is com-ing! and be-fore him powers of darkness must give way;
God is com-ing! fal-ter nev-er—when the conflict here is done

He will de-luge our whole country with his ti-dal wave of love.
Gird your sword and shield about you, and be read-y for the fight.
God is com-ing! by his strong arm we shall gain the vic-tor-y.
You shall wear a crown of glo-ry in the kingdom of his Son.

Chorus.

God is com-ing! pass the watchword all a-long the line to-day!

LET HIM IN.

Rev. J. B. Atchinson.

E. O. Excell.

1. There's a stranger at the door, Let Him in,
2. O - pen now to Him your heart, Let Him in,
3. Hear you now His lov-ing voice? Let Him in,
4. Now ad - mit the heavenly Guest, Let Him in,

Let the Saviour in, let the Saviour in,

He has been there oft be - fore, Let Him in;
If you wait He will de - part, Let Him in;
Now, oh, now make Him your choice, Let Him in,
He will make for you a feast, Let Him in,

Let the Saviour in, let the Saviour in,

Let Him in ere He is gone, Let Him in, the Ho - ly One, Je-sus
Let Him in, He is your Friend, He your soul will sure de-fend, He will
He is standing at the door, Joy to you He will re-store, And His
He will speak your sins forgiv'n, And when earth ties all are riven, He will

Christ, the Father's Son, Let Him in.
keep you to the end, Let Him in.
name you will a - dore, Let Him in.
take you home to heav'n, Let Him in.

Let the Saviour in, let the Saviour in.

40.

HEAVENLY SHEPHERD.

Words and Music by WILBUR A. CHRISTY.

1. The Lord of love   my Shepherd is,   He lead-eth me,
2. My trust-ing soul   He safe - ly guides   For His name's sake,
3. He crowns my head,   gives dai - ly bread,   My heart to cheer,

He lead-eth me   Where pastures grow,   and streamlets flow,
For His name's sake;   And ev' - ry   day   a heavenward way
My heart to cheer!   No cru - el   foe,   nor want nor woe,

CHORUS.

He feed-eth me.   He feed-eth me.   Dear Shepherd, keep   thy trusting
My path doth make,   My path doth make.
Have I   to fear,   Have I to fear.

Dear Shepherd, keep   thy

child;   Be Thou my guard, be Thou my guide,   Till safe with-in

trusting child;   Be Thou my guard,   be Thou my guide,   Till safe within

Rit. ....

Thy heavenly fold,   For-ev - er-more   I shall a - bide.

Thy heavenly fold,   For-ev-er-more   I shall a-bide.

MIGHTY TO SAVE

Words and Music by L. H. BAKER.

41.

1. Trust in the Gracious One, make Him your choice, Trust in the
2. Trust in the Pleading One, His pray'r as-cends, Trust in the
3. Trust in the Sav-ing One, His grace re-ceive, Trust in the

Teaching One, and hear His voice; Trust in the Lov-ing One,
Ho-ly One, He right de-fends; Trust in the Ten-der One,
Faith-ful One, His word be-lieve; Trust in the Ris-in One,

His life He gave, Trust in the Mighty One, might-y to save.
His mer-cy crave, Trust in the Mighty One, might-y to save.
fear not the grave, Trust in the Mighty One, might-y to save.

CHORUS.

Might-y to save (us free-ly), Might-y to save (us ful-ly),

1st. 2d.

Je-sus, the Might-y One, Might-y to save. might-y to save.

SING FOR JOY.

LIZZIE EDWARDS.　　　　　　　　　　　　　　JNO. R. SWENEY, by per.

1. Tidings, happy tidings, Hark! hark! the sound! Hear the joyful ech-o
2. Tidings, happy tidings, Hark! Hark! they say, Do not slight the warning,
3. Tidings, happy tidings, Hark! Hark! again! Rushing o'er the mountain,

Through the world resound; Christ the Lord proclaims them, Hear and heed the call,
Come, O come to-day. Christ, our lov-ing Saviour, still repeats the call—
Sweeping o'er the plain! Onward goes the message, 'Tis the Saviour's call,

REFRAIN.

Come ye starving ones that perish, Room, room for all.　Who-so-ev-er ask-eth,
Come ye wea-ry hea-vy la-den, Room, room for all.
Come for ev-'ry-thing is ready, Room, room for all.

Je-sus will re-ceive; Who-so-ev-er thirsteth, Je-sus will re-lieve.

See the living waters Flowing full and free, O the blessed whosoever, That means me.

A CHILD OF THE KING. 43.

Words by R. E. HUDSON.
Not too fast.

ARRANGED.

1. I know my sins are for - giv - en, My name is writ - ten down,
2. I know that Je - sus loves me, I'm sure I love him too,
3. I'm trust - ing ev' - ry mo - ment, His will is my de - light,

CHO.: *I am a child of the King of kings, His blood now cleans-eth me,*

He's prom-ised me a man - sion, And I shall wear a crown;
And I am rea - dy wait - ing His will and work to do;
My ev' - ry need he doth supply, While walk-ing in the light
I am a child of the King of kings, I now have vic - to - ry;

I know he will be with me In ev' - ry try - ing hour,
I know His pre - cious pro - mise He ne - ver will for - sake;
In fel - low - ship with Je - sus His blood now cleans - eth me;
His love, His peace, His joy are mine; I'm walk-ing in the light;

And I shall have the victo - ry Through his Al - migh - ty power.
He'll guide and guard me ev - er And then at last He'll take.
O glo - ry to his precious name, I'm free, I'm free, I'm free.
I soon shall see Him as He is, Look on His face so bright.

Copyrighted, 1884, by R. E. HUDSON.

44. LOOKING UNTO JESUS.

JAMES NICHOLSON.   By per. WM. G. FISCHER.

1. Looking un-to Je-sus, for sus-tain-ing grace, That I may with patience,
2. Looking un-to Je-sus, when my hopes are bright, Looking unto Je-sus
3. Looking unto Je-sus, when I can-not speak, Looking unto Je-sus
4. Looking unto Je-sus, till the hour shall come, When he sends his angels

run the heavenly race; Looking unto Jesus when I'm weak or strong; Looking unto
when my hopes take flight; Looking unto Jesus when of friends bereft; Looking unto
when my heart would break; Looking unto Jesus, in the darkest hour, Looking unto
down to take me home; Looking unto Jesus, till his face I see, In his unveiled

CHORUS.

Jesus, I am help'd a-long.
Jesus, when there's nothing left.
Jesus, I have peace and power.   Looking unto Je-sus, Looking ev'-ry day,
glory, thro' e-ter-ni-ty.

I have proved that Jesus is the life, the truth, the way. Looking unto Je-sus,

I can nev-er fall, Jesus is my Sav-iour, and my all in all.

MARY D. JAMES.   WARREN W. BENTLEY, By per.

1. In the Rock of A-ges rest-ing, Safely sheltered I a-bide;
2. Long pursued by sin and Sa-tan, Weary, sad, I longed for rest;
3. Peace which passeth un-der-stand-ing, Joy the world can nev er give;
4. In the rift-ed Rock I'll hide me, Till the storms of life are past;

There no foes nor storms mo-lest me, While within the cleft I hide.
Then I found this heav'nly shel-ter, Opened in my Saviour's breast.
Now in Je-sus I am find-ing, In His smiles of love I live.
All se-cure in this blest re-fuge, Heeding not the fiercest blast.

REFRAIN.

Now I'm rest-ing, sweetly rest-ing, In the cleft once made for me;

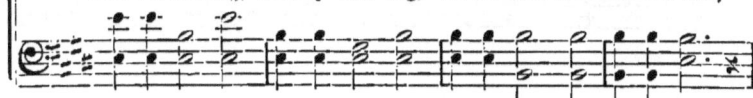

Je-sus, bless-ed Rock of A-ges, I will hide my-self in Thee.

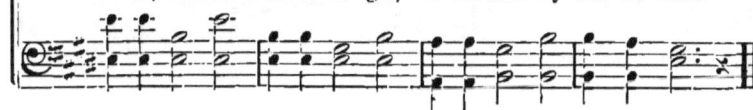

46. SEEK YE THE KINGDOM OF GOD.

(Matt. vi. 33.)

Words and Music by R. E. Hudson.

1. Seek not first for earth-ly treas-ure, Fad-ing joys and worldly pleas-ure,
2. Seek ye first God's peace and blessing, Ye have all if Him possessing,
3. Seek the com-ing of His king-dom, Seek the souls around to win them,

But His love that knows no measure, Seek ye the kingdom of God.
Come, your need and sin confessing, Seek ye the kingdom of God.
Seek to Je-sus Christ to bring them, Seek ye the kingdom of God.

CHORUS.

Seek ye first the kingdom of God, Then you shall reign in yon blissful abode,

Cleansed and made pure in His own precious blood, Oh, seek ye the kingdom of God.

W. A. OGDEN.

W. A. OGDEN, By per.

1. Oh! the cross is all my glo - ry, There I found a per-fect rest;
2. Oh! the cross is all my glo - ry, There my cares and sorrows cease;
3. Oh! the cross is all my glo - ry, To its mighty shade I'll go;

There I laid a-side the bur-den That so long my soul op-pressed.
When the waves of sin are nearing, Then my Saviour speaketh peace.
In the wea - ry day I'll rest me On my pil-grim-age be - low.

CHORUS.

Now I'm rest - ing, sweetly rest-ing, On His breast my head I

Now I'm resting, sweetly rest-ing, On His loving breast my

lay, Je-sus spoke the word of pardon, And my burden rolled away.

head I lay; Jesus spoke the word of pardon, And my burden rolled away.

48. FULL SALVATION.

LOUISE M. ROUSE.   MISS DORA BOOLE.

1. Precious Saviour, thou hast saved me: Thine and only thine I am:
2. Long my yearning heart was trying To en - joy this per - fect rest;
3. Trusting, trusting, ev-ery mo-ment Feeling now the blood ap-plied;
4. Glo - ry to the blood brought me Glo - ry to its cleansing power!

Oh! the cleansing blood has reached me, Glo-ry, glo - ry to the Lamb!
But I gave all try-ing o - ver: Sim-ply trust-ing, I was blest.
Ly-ing at the cleansing fountain; Dwelling in my Sav-iour's side.
Glo - ry to the blood that keeps me! Glo - ry, glo-ry, ev - er - more!

CHORUS.

Glo - ry, glo - ry, Je-sus saves me, Glo - ry, glo - ry, to the Lamb!

Oh! the cleansing blood has reached me, Glo-ry, glo - ry to the Lamb!

HE WILL GATHER THE WHEAT. 49.

HARRIET B. M'KEEVER.   JNO. R. SWENEY.

1. When Je-sus shall gath-er the na-tions Be-fore Him at
2. Shall we hear from the lips of the Sav-iour, The words "Faithful
3. Then let us be watch-ing and wait-ing, Our lamps burn-ing

last to ap-pear, Then, oh, how shall we stand in the judg-ment,
serv-ant, well done;" Or, trembling with fear and with an-guish,
stead-y and bright, When the Bridegroom shall call to the wed-ding,

CHORUS.

When summoned our sentence to hear? He will gath-er the wheat in His
Be banished a-way from His throne?
Our spir-its made ready for flight.

gar-ner, But the chaff will He scat-ter a-way; Then, oh,

how shall we stand in the judg-ment Of the great Re-sur-rec-tion Day?

From "The Garner." by per.

50. SING CF MY REDEEMER.

Words and Music by R. E. HUDSON

1. Sing of His love, His wondrous love, He came from heav'n to die;
2. He came to die that you might live, A - round His throne a-bove,
3. Oh, come, ac-cept His love to - day, He'll wash you white as snow,

On help - less sin - ners lost in sin He looked with pitying eye.
With all the saints in garments white, Filled with His precious love.
His pre cious blood a - lone can cleanse, His word hath told us so.

CHORUS.

Sing of my Re - deem - er, Sing, He died for me;

Sing of my Re-deem-er, Sing of my Re-deem -er, Sing, He died for me, Sing, He died for me,

Sing of my Re-deem - er,

love so free.

Sing of my Redeemer, Sing of my Redeemer, Sing of love so free,

CLINGING TO THE CROSS.

DR. T. C. UPHAM.

J. H. T.

1. O Fath-er, let me bear the cross; Make it my dai-ly food,
2. Take house and lands and earthly fame; To all I am re-sign'd;
3. I know it costs me ma-ny tears, But they are tears of bliss,

Though with it thou dost send the loss Of ev'-ry earth-ly good.
But let me make one earnest claim; Leave, leave the cross behind.
And moments there outweigh the years Of sel-fish hap-pi-ness.

CHORUS.

I am cling-ing, I am cling-ing, Yes, I'm
I am cling-ing to the cross, I am cling-ing to the cross, Yes, I'm

cling-ing to the cross, I am cling-ing, I am
clinging, clinging to the cross, I am cling-ing to the cross, I am

clinging, Yes, I'm cling-ing to the cross.
cling-ing to the cross, Yes, I'm cling-ing to the cross.

From "Songs of Joy," by per.

52. WILL YOU STAND?

Words and Music by R. E. HUDSON.

Firm.

1. Would you stand for Christ in the field for right? Gird the armor on and pre-
2. Will you tell the world of a Saviour's love, How He came to earth from
3. O then stand for Christ in this world of sin; In His strength go forth, dying

pare for the fight; Take the word of God as your shield and chart, It a-
His throne above? How He gave His life on the cross for thee, That
souls you shall win; Be thou strong in God, filled with precious love; By and

CHORUS.
Will you stand?

lone will be a-ble to quench sin's dart.   Will you stand for the
all who believe might thro' Him be free?
by we shall gather round His throne above.

right alone? Will you stand for Christ, Will you make it known? Will you tell of His

Rit.

love where'er you go? Tell His blood, precious blood, cleanseth white as snow?

SAVED TO THE UTTERMOST. 53.

W. J. K.   WM. J. KIRKPATRICK, by per.

1. Saved to the ut - ter-most: I am the Lord's, Je - sus, my Saviour, sal-
2. Saved to the ut - ter-most: Je - sus is near, Keeping me safe - ly, He
3. Saved to the ut - ter-most: this I can say, "Once all was darkness, but
4. Saved to the ut - ter-most: cheerful-ly sing Loud hal - le - lu - jahs to

va - tion af-fords, Gives me His Spir - it, a wit-ness with-in,
cast-eth out fear; Trust-ing His prom - is - es, how I am blest!
now it is day;" Beau-ti-ful vis - ions of glo - ry I see.
Je - sus, my King! Ransomed and pardoned, redeemed by His blood,

CHORUS.

Whisp'ring of par-don, and sav-ing from sin.
Lean-ing up - on Him, how sweet is my rest! Saved, saved, saved to the
Je - sus in brightness revealed un - to me.
Cleansed from unrighteousness, glo - ry to God!

ut - ter-most, Saved, saved by pow - er di - vine! Saved, saved, I'm

saved to the ut - ter - most, Je - sus, the Saviour, is mine.

54. HAVE YOU THE GARMENT OF WHITE?

HARRIET JONES.　　　　　　　　　　　　　　　D. B. TOWNER.

1. The King bids you come and par-take of the feast; For
2. Oh, will you be speech-less when questioned by One, Who
3. Dear friend, are you read-y to meet the great King, And

all there is room ev-en un-to the least; But if you would enter the
of-fered you mer-cy thro' Je-sus, his Son? Who opened a fountain that
join in the anthem the glo-ri-fied sing? Oh, will you be welcome with-

pal-ace so fair; The pure wedding garment you sure-ly must wear.
sin-ners be-low Might wear a bright garment as spot-less as snow?
in that pure home, Where none but the white-robed are suffered to come?

CHORUS.

Oh, have you the garment of white, brother, If called to the banquet to-night—

The beau-ti-ful garment of white, brother, They wear in the palace of light?

BEAUTIFUL HOME.

R. E. HUDSON.

1. They're gathering homeward from every land, One by one, one by one; As
2. Before they may rest they must pass thro' strife, One by one, one by one; Thro'
3. Dear Je - sus, Re-deem-er, our on-ly plea! One by one, one by one; We

wea - ry their feet touch the shin-ing strand, Yes, one by one.
death's chill-ing wa - ters they en - ter life, Yes, one by one.
lift up our voic - es in love to Thee, Yes, one by one.

CHORUS.

Gath - er - ing home, beau - ti-ful home,

Gath-er-ing home, beau-ti-ful home, Beau-ti-ful

Beau - ti-ful home beyond the sky; Gath - er-ing home,

home.......... beyond the sky; Gathering home, beautiful

beau - ti-ful home, We shall meet Him by and by, by and by.

home.

Copyrighted, 1884, by R. E. HUDSON.

56. LILY OF THE VALLEY.

(As sung by Miss Belle McIlfried and Miss Fannie Emmel.)

Arranged by R. E. Hudson.

1. I've found a friend in Je-sus, He's eve-ry-thing to me, He's the
2. He all my griefs has tak-en, And all my sor-rows borne; In temp-
3. He'll nev-er, nev-er leave me, Nor yet for-sake me here, While I

fair-est of ten thousand to my soul; The Lil'-y of the Valley in
ta-tion He's my strong and mighty tow'r; I've all for Him for-sak-en, I've
live by faith and do His bless-ed will; A wall of fire a-bout me, I've

Him a-lone I see, All I need to cleanse and make me ful-ly whole, In
all my i-dols torn From my heart, and now He keeps me by His pow'r; Tho'
noth-ing now to fear; With His manna He my hungry soul shall fill; Then

Cho.—In

sor-row He's my com-fort, in trou-ble He's my stay, He
all the world for-sake me, and Sa-tan tempts me sore, Through
sweeping up to glo-ry to see His bless-ed face, Where

sor-row He's my com-fort, in trou-ble He's my stay; He

tells me eve-ry care on Him to roll. He's the Li-ly of the
Je-sus I shall safe-ly reach the goal. He's the Li-ly of the
riv-ers of de-light shall ev-er flow. He's the Li-ly of the

tells me eve-ry care on Him to roll. He's the Li-ly of the

LILY OF THE VALLEY.—Concluded.

Val-ley, the bright and morning star, He's the fairest of ten thousand to my soul.
Val-ley, the bright and morning star, He's the fairest of ten thousand to my soul.
Val-ley, the bright and morning star, He's the fairest of ten thousand to my soul.

Copyrighted, 1884, by R. E. Hudson.

MARY MAGDALEN. 57.

Arranged by R. E. Hudson.

1. To the hall of the feast came the sinful and fair; She heard in the city that
2. The frown and the murmur went round thro' them all, That one so unhallow'd
   [should
3. She heard but the Saviour; she spoke but with sighs; She dare not look up to the
4. In the sky, after tempest, as shineth the bow, In the glance of the sunbeam

Jesus was there; Unheading the splendor that blazed on the board, She silently
tread in that hall; And some said the poor would be objects more meet, As the
[wealth of her
heav'n of His eyes; And the hot tears gush'd forth at each heave of her breast, As
[her lips to
as melteth the snow He looked on that lost one: "her sins were forgiv'n," And Mary
[went

knelt at the feet of the Lord, She si - lent-ly knelt at the feet of the Lord.
perfume she shower'd on His feet, As the wealth of her perfume she show'red on His
[feet.
His sandals were throbbingly pressed, As her lips to His sandals were throbbingly
[pressed.
forth in the beauty of heav'n, And Mary went forth in the beauty of heav'n.

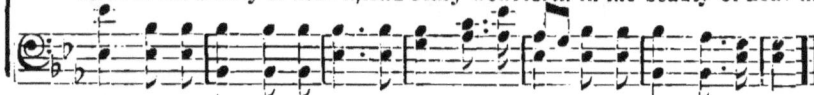

Copyrighted, 1884, by R. E. Hudson.

CHURCH OF GOD, AWAKE.

Mrs. E. J. Bugbee.   T. C. O'Kane, by per.

1. Church of God, whose conquering banners Float along the glorious years,
2. In your cost-ly tem-ples pray-ing, "Let thy kingdom come," ye pray,
3. Grace and glo-ry He hath sent you, Cast your lines in pla-ces fair,

Gath'ring harvest rich and gold-en, Sowed in pov-er-ty and tears:
Are but words of i-dle mean-ing, If with these ye turn a-way;
Scat-ter blessing *now* He bids you, O'er His green earth everywhere;

Onward press, the cross is bend-ing Far to-ward the morning skies,
Boundless wealth to you is giv-en, From His hand who owns it all,
Till the millions in the twi-light Of the far-off O-rient land,

Speedy dawn of light por-tend-ing;—Church of God, a-wake, a-rise!
And His eye beholds in heav-en What ye ren-der back for all.
In the gracious morning splendor Of the Gos-pel light shall stand.

CHORUS.

Church of God, ... awake! a-rise! Christ, your Head... and Master cries,
Church of God, a-wake! arise! Christ, your Head and Master, cries,

CHURCH OF GOD, AWAKE.—Concluded.

Send the Gos - pel's joy-ful sound, Unto-earth's re - mot - est bound.
Oh, send the Gos - pel's joy-ful sound,

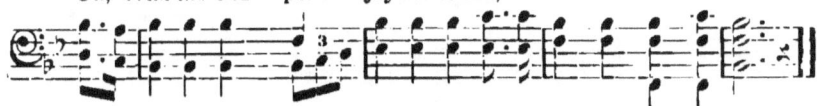

WEIGHED IN THE BALANCE. 59.

Mrs. E. C. Ellsworth.   R. B. Mahaffey.

1. Weigh'd by thy love for thy brother, Weigh'd by thy love for thy God;
2. Weigh'd by the hope of sal - va - tion, Weigh'd by the Rock where 'tis built;
3. Weigh'd by the rich-est of treasures, Weigh'd by their in - fi - nite loss;

Fine.

Weigh'd by thy faith in an - oth-er, Weigh'd by the shedding of blood.
Weigh'd by the sweet in - vi - ta-tion, "Come, e - ven now, if thou wilt."
Weigh'd by the brightest of pleasures, Weigh'd by the dark, heav-y cross.

D.S. *Weigh'd, but thy soul has been trifling, Weigh'd, but found lighter than air.*

REFRAIN.

60. WHO SHALL BE ABLE?

K. S.

KNOWLES SHAW, by per.

1. When the trump of God shall sound, And the nations gather round, And the
2. When the deluge swept the world, And to death its millions hurled, And the
3. When the cit-ies of the plain Were enveloped in the flame, And de-
4. When the day of wrath is come, And the day of mercy gone, And to

Judge shall sit up-on the roy-al throne: Who will hear the welcome word
wa-ters covered o-ver all the land; Those who trusted in the Lord,
struction swept the mul-ti-tudes a-way; There was just a lit-tle band
judgment they are called from every land; Sin-ner, how is it with thee?

From the lips of Christ, the Lord, "En-ter in, good and faithful with my own."
And obeyed His holy word, These were all that were able then to stand.
Who were a-ble then to stand In that great and that lawful judgment day.
Christian, how then shall it be: Shall we all there be a-ble then to stand?

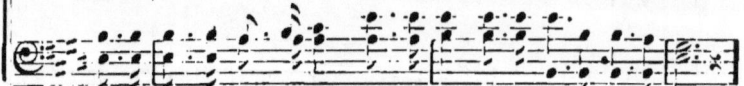

CHORUS.

Who shall be a-ble then to stand? Who shall be a-ble

shall be a-ble then to stand?

then to stand? All who trust in Christ, the Lord, And o-

shall be a-ble then to stand?

bey His ho - ly word: These shall be a - ble then to stand.

HE WOULD NOT GO AWAY. 61.

J. W. McABEE.

1. I nev - er was puz-zled be-fore, As I was up - on that day, When
2. I did not want Him to go, I could not ask Him to stay, What
3. I feared to let Him in, Things were in such a state; Could

Cho.—Oh, come to the Saviour now, Where sin-ners are forgiven; Oh,

Je - sus stood at my door—And would not go a - way.
to do I did not know, He would not go a - way.
I get read - y for Him, If He would on - ly wait!

come to the Sav-iour now, And go with me to heaven.

4 I thought in time I might
  With some of my sins make way,
  Or hide them out of sight—
  But He would not go away.

5 Mine eyes with tears were dim,
  And all the night and day
  I could only think of Him,
  For He would not go away.

6 At last I ceased to weep,
  Then I forgot to pray,
  The door of my heart I could not keep,
  I asked Him in to stay.

  Chorus after last verse.
  He is my Saviour now,
  My sins are all forgiven;
  He is my Saviour now,
  I'm on my way to heaven.

PEACE DIVINE.

I. N. McHose.

1. God's al-might-y arms are round me, Peace is mine, peace di-vine;
2. Tho' life's o-cean wild-ly roll-eth, Peace is mine, peace di-vine:
3. Wel-come ev'-ry ris-ing sun-light, Peace is mine, peace di-vine;

Cares of life may not confound me, Peace is mine, peace di-vine;
Winds and waves our God con-troll-eth, Peace is mine, peace di-vine;
Near-er home in ev'-ry midnight, Peace is mine, peace di-vine;

Je-sus came him-self and sought me, To His lov-ing fold He brought me,
I can sing with Christ be-side me, Tho' a thousand ills be-tide me,
Death and hell can-not ap-pall me, Safe in Christ whate'er be-fall me,

Bless-ed free-dom Je-sus taught me, Ev-er-last-ing peace is mine.
He will safe-ly keep and guide me, Ev-er-last-ing peace is mine.
Calm-ly wait I 'till He call me, Ev-er-last-ing peace is mine.

CHORUS.

Peace is mine,...... peace is mine,..... Ev-er-last - ing peace is mine;
'Tis mine,   'Tis mine,

PEACE DIVINE.—Concluded.

Peace is mine,... sweet peace is mine, Ev-er - last - ing peace is mine.

'Tis mine,

WE SHALL SING.

E. N. **63.**

1. Soldiers fight-ing in the bat-tle. Up to glo-ry march a-long; Keeping
2. Sing to-day, and sing to-morrow, Sing when things are going wrong; Sing the
3. Use the joy that God has giv-en, For the battle keeping strong; Liv-ing

CHORUS.

cheerful in the struggle, Praise the Lord, it won't be long. We shall sing,
most in pain or sorrow; Praise the Lord, it won't be long.
near the gate of heaven; Praise the Lord, it won't be long.

We shall

We shall sing When the glorious fight of faith is

sing, We shall sing,

o - ver, Round the tree of life for-ev - er, Praise the Lord, it won't be long.

64.

CALVARY.

Dedicated to Miss Belle McIlfried and Miss Fanny Emmel.

R. E. HUDSON.

1. Once I was bound............ .... by sin's dark chain,........ ...... And
2. I heard a voice.................... which sweetly said :................. "Come
3. This heart once dark,.................. now filled with light,................. Bathed
4. O wea-ry one,.................... come un-to me! .... He'll

far a-way... .... from God I strayed;............... And
un-to me. .... and be at rest!"................... My
in the blood......... ...... of Christ, my King· .... And
free-ly par - - don all thy sin:............... ... O

on be-fore..................... an aw-ful doom,...... .... And
blood was for..................... thy ran-som shed,"............ And
in the peace.................... that fills my heart............... Shouts
hear Him say.................. those words of joy:.. .... "Who

yet my soul.................... was not a-fraid...................
now with par - - don I am blest...................
forth His prais - - es, and I sing...................
ev-er will.................... may en-ter in."...................

CALVARY.—Concluded.

CHORUS.

O Cal-va-ry, dark Cal-va-ry, Where Jesus shed His blood for me; O
Cal-va-ry, dark Cal-va-ry, Speak to my heart and set me free.

REDEEMED. 65.

Words and music by R. E. HUDSON.

1. Redeemed from the law I had brok-en, Redeemed, Redeemed; Re-
2. Redeemed, and by faith I'm for-giv-en, Redeemed, Redeemed; My
3. Redeemed, O I'll tell the glad sto-ry, Redeemed, Redeemed; And

Cho.—Redeemed, how I love to pro-claim it! Redeemed, Redeemed; Re-

Repeat for Chorus.

deemed, for my Saviour hath spok-en, Redeemed by the blood of the Lamb.
name is now writ-ten in Heav-en, Redeemed by the blood of the Lamb.
soon I'll be with Him in glo-ry, Redeemed by the blood of the Lamb.

deemed, how I love to pro-claim it! Redeemed by the blood of the Lamb.

CLEANSING BALM.

R. K. C.   R. KELSO CARTER, By per.

1. Oh! come to the cross where Je-sus bled and died, Oh! come to the
2. He's a - ble to save from all the guilt of sin, He's a - ble to
3. He's will-ing to save, to seek and save the lost, He's will - ing to
4. He does save me now from eve-ry act of sin, He does save me

cross where He was cru - ci - fied; Oh! come to the cross, 'tis
save from all that's born with-in; He's a - ble to save by
save the Christian, tempest-tossed; He's will - ing to save, so
now from eve-ry spot with-in; He does save me now, He

finished there, He cried! For the blood of Je - sus cleanseth us from all sin.
sim-ple faith in Him, For the blood of Je - sus cleanseth us from all sin.
free - ly with-out cost, For the blood of Je - sus cleanseth us from all sin.
makes and keeps me clean, For the blood of Je - sus cleanseth *me* from all sin.

REFRAIN.

There is balm   in Gi - lead,   balm   in
There is precious balm in Gi - lead, there is heal - ing balm in

Gi - lead, There is balm   in Gi - lead for the soul that needeth
Gi - lead, There is per - fect balm in Gi - lead for the soul that needeth

CLEANSING BALM.—Concluded.

cleansing; Sing praise   to   Je - sus,   praise   to
cleansing; Sing praise,sing praise to Je - sus, oh! sing praise,sing praise to

Je - sus, Sing praise   to   Je - sus, Oh! glo - ry   to   His name.
Je-sus,Sing praise,sing praise to Je - sus, Oh! glo - ry   to   His name.

STAY, SINNER, STAY.   67.

Slow.   Arranged by R. E. H.

1. Stay, sin - ner, stay! the night comes on, When slighted mer - cy is with-
2. Stay, sin - ner, stay! 'tis Je - sus pleads, For you He weeps,for you He
3. Come,sinner,come! tho' guil - ty now, At Je · sus' feet sub-mis-sive
4. See! sin - ner, see! where loved ones stand, All saved in heav'n—a hap-py

drawn; The Holy Spirit strives no more, And Jesus gives His pleadings o'er-
bleeds; Oh,let His love your hearts constrain,Nor let Him weep and bleed in vain!
bow. And freely all shall be forgiv'n; Oh, come and taste the joys of heav'n!
band; Oh,come and join them on that shore,Where death and parting are no more.

68. 'NEATH THE SHADOW OF HIS WING.

Rev. W. E. Penn. I. Baltzell.

Moderato.

1. When darkness gathers o'er my soul, My heart so sad it cannot sing,
2. Dark waves may roll, the tempests roar, Earthquakes and wars their terrors bring,
3. There is no pow'r beneath the sun, Not ev-en death's cold icy sting,
4. Then, sin-ner, come, O quickly come, Take Jesus as your Priest and King!

'Tis sweet to know that there is rest Be-neath the shadow of His wing.
But all is safe if I am found Be-neath the shadow of His wing.
Can ev-er reach the soul that rests Be-neath the shadow of His wing.
That you this blessed rest may find Be-neath the shadow of His wing.

CHORUS.

I am rest - - ing, sweet-ly rest - -
I am rest-ing, sweet-ly rest-ing, I am rest-ing, sweet-ly

ing, And my heart his prais-es sing; Rest-ing in the
rest-ing.

love of Je-sus, 'Neath the shad-ow of His wing.

Rev. W. T. Dale. D. E. Dortch, by per.

1. Just waiting the summons to welcome me home, Just waiting the time when my
2. Just waiting to step from the borders of time, Just waiting to enter the
3. Just waiting to stand on the beautiful shore, With kindred and friends who have

Saviour shall come To take me away to his palace on high, And give me
heavenly clime, Just waiting the fi - nal a-dieu here below, Just waiting
gone on before, Just waiting to sing with the an-gels above, Just waiting

Wait - ing, yes, wait - ing, just

a place with the saints in the sky.
with Jesus, my Saviour, to go. Waiting, yes, waiting, waiting, yes, waiting, just
to chant the sweet anthem of love.

Wait - ing, yes,

wait - ing 'till Je-sus, my Saviour, shall come; Waiting, yes, waiting, yes,

wait - ing, just wait-ing,

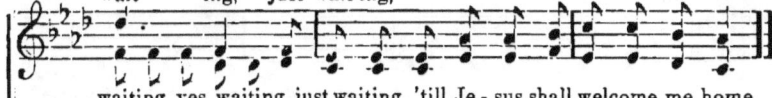

waiting, yes, waiting, just waiting, 'till Je - sus shall welcome me home.

70. DON'T BE TOO LATE.

Words and Music arranged by R. E. Hudson.

1. There is a land of pure de-light, Where saints im-mor-tal reign;
2. There ev - er - last-ing spring a-bides, And nev - er - with'ring flowers:
3. Sweet fields be-yond the swell-ing flood, Stand dressed in liv-ing green;

In - fi - nite day excludes the night, And pleas-ures ban - ish pain.
Death, like a nar - row sea di-vides This heavenly land from ours.
So to the Jews old Ca - naan stood, While Jordan rolled be - tween.

CHORUS.

Then be pre - pared, to pass through the gol-den gate.

Then be pre-pared to pass through the gold-en gate.

He now in - vites, O come ere it be too late.

He now in-vites, O come ere it be too late.

SOLO ALTO.

Is there an-y-one here who is not prepared to en-ter that golden gate?

Solo Alto.

How sad it would be to hear him say, too late to en - ter the gate.

Duet.—Tenor and Alto.

'Don't let it be said, too late, too late, to en - ter that gold - en gate;

Be read - y, for soon the time will come, How sad it would be if too late.

Chorus.

That beau - ti - ful gold - en gate, That beau - ti - ful gold - en gate,

Be read - y for soon the time will come, How sad it would be if too late.

72. I WILL GIVE YOU REST.

AMICUS.

I. BALTZELL.

1. Come, wea-ry soul, sin-burdened and distressed, Je-sus now waits to
2. See mer-cy's boundless wa-ters free-ly flow, To cleanse thy heart and
3. Haste, sin-ner, haste, while mercy may be found, Soon may be hushed the
4. Je-sus, I come, O help my un-be-lief! Now I am trust-ing,

give the promised rest; Hast-en, O wanderer, at His footstool bow;
ban-ish eve-ry woe; Par-don and peace and end-less life He'll give,
Gos-pel's joy-ous sound; Hear Je-sus say to eve-ry soul oppressed:
give my soul re-lief! Wash me, O Sav-iour, in thy cleansing blood,

CHORUS.
Tenderly.

On-ly be-lieve Him, He will save you now.
On-ly be-lieve Him, on-ly look and live. Come un-to me,
"Come un-to me, and I will give you rest."
Seal me thine own, O precious Lamb of God.

Rit. ad lib.

come un-to me, Come un-to me and I will give you rest.

SAVED BY HIS GRACE ALONE! 73.

DUET.—Soprano & Tenor.   L. H. Baker.

1. Grace! 'tis a charming sound,......   Harmonious to the ear;......
2. Grace first contrived a way.........   To save re-bell-ious man;......
3. Grace taught my roving feet.........   To tread the heavenly road;......
4. Grace all the work shall crown,...... Thro' ev-er-last-ing days;......

Heaven with the ech-o shall resound, And all the earth shall hear.
And all the steps that grace dis-play Which drew the wondrous plan.
And new supplies each hour I meet, While pressing on to God.
It lays in heaven the top-most stone, And well deserves our praise.

CHORUS.

Saved by His grace a - lone!.........   Saved by His grace a - lone!

Saved   by His grace a-lone! Saved by His grace, by His grace alone!

And we shall sing a-round His throne: Saved by His grace a-lone!

74.

R. E. HUDSON.

HE IS COMING.

Arranged by R. E. H.

DUET.—Soprano and Tenor.

1. { He is com - ing by and by, I shall see Him
   { I shall join the blood-washed throng, I shall sing the

2. { I shall see Him as he is, O what rap - ture
   { Cleansed and clothed in spot-less white, Ev - er walk - ing

3. { Are you read - y when He comes? Have you in your
   { He will come and reign with-in, He will cleanse your

as He is, All the sor - rows of this life be o'er, }
new, new song, I shall reign with Him for - ev - er - more. }
and what bliss! I shall see my Sa - viour and a - dore, }
in the light, I shall sing of Him for - ev - er - more. }
heart made room For the King of glo - ry to a - bide? }
heart from sin, Then with Him the soul is sat - is - fied. }

CHORUS.

He is com - - ing by and by, He will

He is com-ing by and by, He is com-ing by and by; He is

come............. and claim His own; He is com - ing

come and claim His own; H will come and claim His own; He is coming by and by,

by and by, We shall gath - er round His throne.

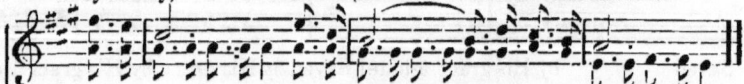

He is coming by and by, We shall gather, hallelujah! We shall gather round His
[throne.

THERE IS LIFE IN A LOOK. 75.

Rev. J. Parker.

By per. S. J. Vail.

1. There is life in a look at the cru - ci - fied One, And
2. There is peace in a look at the cru - ci - fied One, He
3. There is rest in a look at the cru - ci - fied One, When

joy to the spir - it with - in; There is pardon for thee, sin - ner,
bore all my bur - den and shame; I have nothing to bring, To His
wea - ry I fly to His care; He in - vites me to come, In His

REFRAIN.

come and be free, For His blood giveth cleansing from sin.
mer - cy I cling, I am trusting a - lone in His name. Oh, trust in His
love there is room, And I'm welcome His mercy to share.

own precious blood, Who gives us acceptance with God; He has pardoned

my sin, And renewed me with - in, I love Him and trust in His word.

76. LIVING WATERS FLOW.

Respectfully dedicated to Miss Ida L. Mulleniz.

R. E. HUDSON.

1. I've reached the land of light, The air is pure and bright, Down where the living
2. I've reached the land of rest, While trusting I am blest, Down where the living
3. I've reached the land of joy, I've love without al-loy, Down where the living

wa-ters flow; For God and souls I fight, I'm do-ing what is right,
wa-ters flow; Peace, like a riv-er, rolls, And love it fills my soul,
wa-ters flow; I rest in Him complete, While sitting at His feet,

CHORUS.

Down where the liv-ing wa-ters flow.
Down where the liv-ing wa-ters flow.   Down where the living waters flow,
Down where the liv-ing wa-ters flow.

Down where the tree of life doth grow,   I'm walk-ing in the light; For

God and souls I fight, Down where the liv - ing wa-ters flow.

CAST THY BURDEN ON THE LORD. 77.

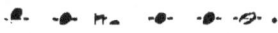

L. H. B.

L. H. BAKER.

1. Child of God, in serv-ice faith-ful, Does thy du-ty seem a
2. He will com-fort and sus-tain thee, He will strength and help af-
3. Cast-ing all your care up-on Him, He will guide you by His

load? (heavy load?) Hear these words of love e - ter - nal: "Cast thy
ford; (help afford;) He will light-en ev'-ry du-ty; Cast thy
word; (faithful word;) He will gladden hearts that trust Him; Cast thy

CHORUS.

burden on the Lord."   Cast thy bur - den on the Lord,...
burden on the Lord.
burden on the Lord.

CHURCH RALLYING SONG.

Fanny J. Crosby.   Jno. R. Sweney.

1. A - wake! awake! the Mas-ter now is call-ing us, A-rise! a-rise! and,
2. A cry for light from dy-ing ones in heathen lands: It comes, it comes a-
3. O church of God, ex-tend thy kind, ma-ter-nal arms To save the lost on

trust-ing in His word, Go forth, go forth! proclaim the year of ju-bi-lee, And
cross the ocean's foam; Then haste, oh, hast to spread the words of truth abroad, For-
mountains dark and cold, Reach out thy hand with loving smile to rescue them, And

CHORUS.

take the cross, the blessed cross of Christ, our Lord.   On, on, swell the
get - ing not the starving poor at home, dear home.   On, on, on,
bring them to the shel - ter of the Saviour's fold.   On, on, on,

cho - rus;   On,   on, the morning star   is shin-ing o'er us;
swell the cho - rus,   On, on, on,

On, on, while be-fore   us Our mighty, mighty Saviour leads the way:
On, on, on,   while before   leads the way:

CHURCH RALLYING SONG.—Concluded.

{ Glo - ry, glo-ry, hear the ev - er-last-ing throng }
{ Shout ho-san-na, while we boldly march a-long; } Faithful soldiers here below,

On-ly Je-sus will we know, Shouting "free salvation" o'er the world we go.

REJOICING EVERMORE. 79.

R. E. HUDSON.

1. Though troubles as - sail, and dan - gers affright, Tho' friends should all
2. When Sa - tan ap - pears to stop up our path, And fills us with
3. He tells us we're weak—our hope is in vain; The good that we

CHO.— Yes, I will re - joice, re - joice in the Lord, Yes, I will re-

fail, and foes all u - nite, Yet one thing secures us, whatev - er be-
fears, we tri - umph by faith; He can-not take from us (tho' oft He has
seek we ne'er shall obtain; But when such suggestions our graces have

joice, re-joice in the Lord, Yes, I will re-joice, re-joice in the

tide, The prom-ise as - sures us,—The Lord will pro - vide.
tried) The heart-cheering promise,—The Lord will pro - vide.
tried, This answers all questions,—The Lord will pro - vide.

Lord, Will joy in the God of my sal - va - tion.

80. HEAR HIM CALLING.

MRS. M. B. C. SLADE.   DR. A. D. EVERETT.

1. Are you stay-ing, safe-ly stay-ing In the ten-der Shepherd's
2. Are you hear-ing, glad-ly hear-ing, How He bids his fold-ed
3. Are you roam-ing, long-er roam-ing, In the cold, dark night of

peaceful folds? No, I'm stray-ing, sad-ly stray-ing, On the
flock re-joice? No, I'm fear-ing, sad-ly fear-ing, I have
doubt and sin? No, I'm com-ing, quick-ly com-ing! O-pen

REFRAIN.

lone-ly mountains dark and cold.
followed far the stranger's voice.   On your ear His lov-ing tones are
door, make hast to let me in!

pp

fall-ing, For He seeks you, where-so-e'er you roam; Hear Him call-ing,

sweet-ly call-ing, As He bids His wand'ring child come home.

By permission of R. M. MCINTOSH.

R. E. HUDSON.

1. A - las! and did my Sav - iour bleed, And did my Sovereign die,
2. Was it for crimes that I have done, He groaned up-on the tree?
3. But drops of grief can ne'er re - pay The debt of love I owe;

Would He de-vote that sa-cred head For such a worm as I?
A - maz - ing pit - y, grace unknown, And love be - yond de-gree!
Here, Lord, I give my - self a - way, 'Tis all that I can do!

CHORUS.

At the cross, at the cross, where I first saw the light, And the

bur - den of my heart rolled a - way—   It was there by faith

rolled away,

I re-ceived my sight, And now I am hap - py all the day.

82. FOR YOU AND FOR ME.

Very slow.

Words and Music by WILL. L. THOMPSON.

1. Soft - ly and ten - der - ly Je - sus is call - ing,— Call - ing for
2. Why should we tar - ry when Je - sus is pleading,— Pleading for
3. O for the won - der - ful love He has promised,— Promised for

you and for me; See, on the por - tals He's wait-ing and
you and for me? Why should we ling - er and heed not His
you and for me; Though we have sinned, He has mer-cy and

REFRAIN.

watching,— Watching for you and for me. Come home,...... come
mer - cies,— Mer-cies for you and for me? Come home,
par - don,— Par - don for you and for me.

cres.   *rit.*   *p*   *pp*

home,...... Ye, who are wea-ry, come home;... Earn est - ly;
come home,

ritard.   *pp*

ten-der - ly, Je-sus is call-ing,— Call-ing, O sin-ner, come home.

TO-MORROW IT MAY BE TOO LATE. 83.

E. A. Hoffman.   Albert Hook, by per.

DUET. Earnestly.

1. Now is the time to seek the Lord! Before this Sabbath's setting sun Has
2. Now is the time to seek the Lord! Before night's sable curtains drop Thy
3. Now is the time to seek the Lord! While yet th Saviour strives within, Oh,
4. Now is the time to seek the Lord! Beyond the dark and narrow grave No

sunk   behind the west-ern hills, Thine earth-ly jour - ney may be run.
soul may leave the frame of clay, The beat - ings of   thy heart may stop.
yield thy heart to His free grace, And let Him cleanse thee from thy sin.
mer - cy lights the dis-mal gloom, No Sav - iour there thy soul to save!

CHORUS.

Come now   to Christ,   Come now, why will   you long - er

Come now   to Christ, Come now, why will   you long - er

wait? Come now   to Christ,   To-morrow it may be too late!

wait?   Come now   to Christ, To-morrow it may be too late!

84. GLORY TO CHRIST, MY KING!

R. E. HUDSON.

L. H. BAKER.

1. Oh, tell the sto - ry o'er and o'er, Of love so full and free;
2. He died for me, naught but His love, Could melt this heart of mine;
3. His life, His death, His precious love, To you shall all be given;

I give my-self, my all to Him, Who bled and died for me.
Oh, come and take this prec-ious gift, Of peace and joy di - vine.
Come now, ac-cept His offered grace, And reign with Him in heaven.

CHORUS.

Oh, won - - der - ful Sav - iour!

Oh, won-der-ful, won-der-ful Sav-iour! His prais-es I will sing;

Oh, won - der-ful Sav - iour!

Oh, won-der-ful, won-der-ful Sav-iour! All glo - ry to Christ, my King!

COME AND HELP US.

H. B. HARTZLER.   ALBERT HOOK, by per.

Allegro.

1. Come and help us, friends of Je - sus, Come and share the faithful toil,
2. Come and help us, we are fee - ble, And the reap - er - band is small—
3. Come and help us work for Je - sus, For the love He bore to you;
4. Come and help us, if you love Him; Ho-ly work will make you strong,
5. Come and help us, we are wea-ry; Give us words of hope and cheer;

From the wrecks of sin and sor-row, Help us gath-er precious spoil.
Oh, the fields of wav-ing harv-est, How they ech-o Je - sus' call!
Give Him back in true de - vo-tion What He bought with blood a-new.
Bring you near - er to the Mas - ter, Tune your soul to sweeter song.
Help to bear the heat and bur-den, Till the great reward ap - pear.

Obligato Duet.—1st & 2d. SOPRANO.

Come and help us, Come and help us, Come and help us, friends of

Je-sus, Come and help us, Come and help, Friends of Jesus, Come and help.

CHORUS.

Come, come, come, Come and help us, Come, come, come, Friends of Jesus,

Come, come, come, Come and help us, Friends of Je - sus, Come and help.

86. LEAD ME SAFELY ON.

J. H. LESLIE.   R. A. GLENN, by per.

1. Lead me safe-ly on by the nar-row way, From the shores of
2. With a Shepherd's care thro' the night and day, Keep me close to
3. Thro' the storms of life, 'mid the o-cean's foam, Lead me safe-ly

time to the realms of day; By the cross of Christ may I
thee lest I go a-stray; Lead me safe-ly on by thy
on to my heaven-ly home; At the fount of life on the

ev - er stand, As I jour-ney on to the bet-ter land.
tend - er love, Thro' this world of sin to my home a-bove.
oth - er shore, Let me free-ly drink till I thirst no more.

REFRAIN.

Lead me on,   lead me on,   Lead me

Lead me on,   lead me on, By the straight and narrow way,

on,   lead me on,

Lead me on,   lead me on To the realms of end-less day.

Dedicated to W. C. T. U. of the United States. R. E. HUDSON.

1. Lo! the night of ease is past, Ac - tion comes, in love, at last,
2. It has filled our hap - py land With its wrecks on ev -'ry hand,
3. Ye who pi - ty, ye who feel, Lis - ten now to our ap - peal,
4. Un - to Thee we look for power, Help us in this cri - sis hour,

As we hail the dawning day; Who shall roll the stone a - way?
While the helpless vic - tims pray, Roll this dreadful stone a - way.
All who sym - pathize and pray, Help us roll the stone a - way.
Bring the dawning of the day, Roll, oh, roll the stone a - way.

CHORUS. Roll......... the stone a - way,

Roll the stone, the stone a - way, Brothers, roll, while sis - ters pray,

Join to - geth - er heart and hand, And roll the stone a - way.

88.

1 Children of the heavenly King,
As we journey let us sing,
Sing our Saviour's worthy praise,
Glorious in his works and ways.

2 We are traveling home to God,
In the way our Father's trod;
They are happy now, and we
Soon their happiness shall see.

3 Fear not, brethren, joyful stand
On the borders of our land;
Jesus Christ, our Father's Son,
Bids us undismayed go on.

4 Lord! obediently we'll go,
Gladly leaving all below;
Only thou our Leader be,
And we still will follow thee.

89. RING, RING THE BELLS.

Words and Music by R. E. HUDSON.

1. Christmas bells are ring-ing, Mer-ry bells, joy-ful bells,
2. Christmas bells are ring-ing, Peace on earth, good news bring,
3. Christmas bells are ring-ing, Heav'n-ly bells, earth-ly bells,

Hap-py news are bring-ing, Je-sus is our King!
Chil-dren now are sing-ing, Je-sus is our King!
Love and peace are bring-ing, Je-sus is our King!

CHORUS.

Ring, ring the bells,
Ring, ring, Ring, ring the bells, Glad good news to earth they bring;

Ring, ring the bells,
Ring, ring, Ring, ring the bells, Je-sus is our King!

90. MARCHING TO ZION.

1 Come, ye that love the Lord,
  And let your joys be known;
  Join in a song with sweet accord,
  While ye surround His throne.

CHO.—We're marching to Zion,
  Beautiful, beautiful Zion!
  We're marching upward to Zion,
  The beautiful city of God.

2 Oh watch, and fight, and pray,
  The battle ne'er give o'er;
  Renew it boldly every day,
  And help divine implore.

3 Ne'er think the vict'ry won,
  Nor lay thine armor down;
  The work of faith will not be done,
  Till thou obtain the crown.

I WILL TRUST.

C. WESLEY.
By per. T. C. O'KANE.

1. For - ev - er here my rest shall be, Close to thy bleed-ing side;
2. My dy - ing Sav-iour and my God, Fountain for guilt and sin,
3. Wash me, and make me thus thine own: Wash me, and mine thou art;

This all my hope and all my plea, For me the Sav-iour died.
Sprin-kle me ev - er with thy blood, And cleanse, and keep me clean.
Wash me, but not my feet a - lone, My hands, my head, my heart.

CHORUS.

I will trust, I will trust, I will trust in the blood of the Lamb; I will

trust, I will trust, I will trust in the blood of the Lamb.

I WILL GUIDE THEE. 92.

1 Precious promise God hath given
To the weary passer by,
On the way from earth to heaven,
"I will guide thee with Mine eye."
REF—I will guide thee, I will guide thee,
I will guide thee with Mine eye;
On the way from earth to heaven
I will guide thee with Mine eye.

When temptations almost win thee,
And thy trusted watchers fly;
Let this promise ring within thee,
"I will guide thee with Mine eye."
When the shades of life are falling,
And the hour has come to die ;
Hear thy trusty pilot calling,
"I will guide thee with Mine eye."

93. PERFECT PEACE.

Dedicated to my friends, Samuel Sechrist and wife, of Warsaw, Ind.

Slow.

Words and Music by R. E. HUDSON.

1. Peace, sweet peace, Peace that passeth understanding, Perfect peace that has no
2. Perfect love, Perfect love all fear removing, Fills the heart, all sorrows
3. Joy, joy, joy, Joy to know my sins forgiven, Cleansed, made pure, prepar'd for

ending, Peace, that like a river deepens, Till we reach the pearly gates.
soothing, Dwells in God the fountain flowing, Till we join the blood-washed throng.
heaven, Evermore in Him rejoicing, Till my work on earth is o'er.

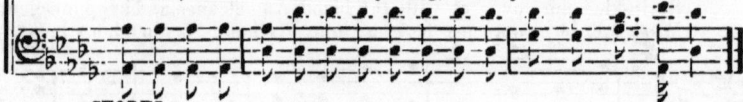

CHORUS.

Perfect peace,　　Perfect peace,　　Oh, what joy to know I'm saved,

Perfect peace,　Perfect peace,

Cleansed from sin, Pure with-in,　Oh, for me His life He gave.

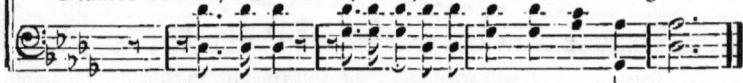

Cleansed from sin, Pure within,

Music for this Hymn, No. 61 Gems of Gospel Song.

94.

1. Blessed assurance, Jesus is mine!
Oh, what a foretaste of glory divine!
Heir of salvation, purchased of God,
Born of his Spirit, washed in his blood.

Cho.–This is my story, this is my song,
Praising my Saviour all the day long;
This is my story, this is my song,
Praising my Saviour all the day long.

Copyrighted, 1884, by R. E. Hudson.

2. Perfect submission, perfect delight,
Visions of rapture burst on my sight;
Angels descending bring from above,
Echoes of mercy, whispers of love.

3. Perfect submission, all is at rest,
I in my Saviour am happy and blest;
Watching and waiting, looking above.
Filled with his goodness, lost in his love.

Words and Music by R. E. Hudson.

Slow.

1. Je-sus is waiting, dear sin-ner,   Wait-ing to save you from sin,
2. Je-sus is seeking you, sin-ner,   Seek-ing by night and by day ;
3. Je-sus is knocking, my brother,   Why will you turn Him a-way?

Plead-ing His blood, O how precious!   Wait-ing to welcome you in.
Long-ing to hear you say welcome,   Turning from all sin a-way.
Je-sus in mer-cy is pleading,   Why will you longer de-lay?

CHORUS.

Wait-ing, wait-ing, Je-sus has bid-den you come;

Wait-ing, wait-ing, wand'rer, O wand'rer, come home.

Copyrighted, 1884, by R. E. Hudson.

WHAT A FRIEND WE HAVE IN JESUS. 96.

1 What a friend we have in Jesus,
  All our sins and griefs to bear !
What a privilege to carry
  Every thing to God in prayer!
Oh, what peace we often forfeit,
  Oh, what endless pain we bear--
All because we do not carry
  Every thing to God in prayer.

2 Have we trials and temptations?
  Is there trouble anywhere ?
We should never be discouraged,
  Take it to the Lord in prayer ;
Can we find a friend so faithful,
  Who will all our sorrows share?
Jesus knows our every weakness ;
  Take it to the Lord in prayer.

97. HE KNOWS.

Slow with Expression. Words and Music by R. E. HUDSON.

1. He knows, He knows, He knows, He knows my frame, that I am
2. He knows, He knows, He knows, He knows I long to love Him
3. He knows, He knows, He knows, He knows I long to do His

dust, He knows my heart in Him I trust, He knows what sore
more To tell the story o'er and o'er: Of cleans-ing blood,
will, He knows His love my heart doth fill, He knows His joy

temp-ta - tions are: He knows I love Him, trust His care,
of sav - ing pow'r, Of vic - t'ry in each con - flict hour.
His peace is mine, He knows I all to Him re - sign.

98. WE'LL PRESS THIS BATTLE ON.

R. E. HUDSON.

1. A charge to keep I have, A God to glo - ri - fy;
2. Help me to watch and pray, And on thy-self re - ly,

Chorus:— We'll press this bat-tle on, We'll press this bat - tle on,

A nev - er - dy - ing soul to save, And fit it for the sky.
As-sured, if I my trust be-tray, I shall for - ev - er die.
In Je-sus' might we'll stand and fight, And press this bat-tle on.

WE'LL WORK. 99.

1. { Am I a soldier of the cross, A follower of the Lamb? ....
{ And shall I fear to own his cause, ... Or blush to speak his name.
2. { Must I be carried to the skies On flowery beds of ease, ..., ...
{ While others fought to win the prize, ... And sailed thro' bloody seas?
3. { Since I must fight, if I would reign, Increase my courage, Lord! ....
{ I'll bear the toil, endure the pain, ... Supported by thy word.

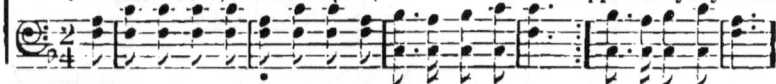

CHORUS.

We'll work, we'll work till Je-sus comes, We'll work till Je-sus comes;

We'll work, we'll work till Je-sus comes, And we'll be gathered home.

I LOVE THEE. 100.

|1st. |2d. :S:

1. { My Je-sus, I love Thee, I know Thou art mine, ... My gra -
{ For Thee all the pleasures of sin I .... re-sign; If ev -
There's no

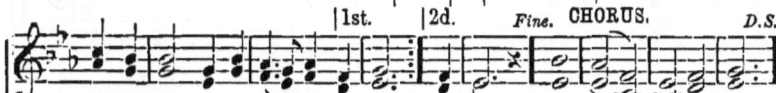

|1st. |2d. *Fine.* **CHORUS.** D.S.

cious Redeemer, my Saviour art Thou, ... } Home, Home, sweet, sweet
er I loved Thee, my Je-sus, ... 'tis now. } [Home,
friend like Je-sus, There's no place like Home.

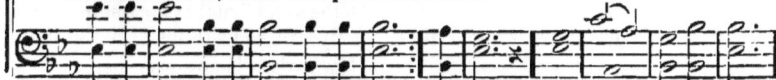

2 I love Thee because Thou hast first loved me,
And purchased my pardon when nailed to the tree;
I love Thee for wearing the thorns on Thy brow,
If ever I loved Thee, my Jesus, 'tis now.

101. TAKE MY HAND, DEAR JESUS.

KATE OSBORN.

WM. W. BENTLEY, By per.

1. Ev - er blessed Je - sus, Listen un - to me, Bow thine ear and hear me,
2. Ever blessed Jesus, Bless Thy wayward child, Keep my feet from straying
3. Help me, blessed Jesus, Leave me not alone, Give me strength and patience,

While I call to thee ; I am weak and sin-ful, Thou art pure and strong ;
Through the de-sert wild ; I would never wander From Thy lov-ing side,
Till each du-ty's done ; And when life is ended, I Thy face would see,

CHORUS.

Take my hand, dear Je-sus, Lead thy child along.
Ev - er bless - ed Je-sus, Be my constant guide. Take my hand, dear Jesus,
Hear my pray'r, dear Jesus, Take me up to Thee.

Let me nev-er stray, Take my hand and lead me in the bet-ter way.

102. OVER THERE.

1 Oh! think of the home over there,
By the side of the river of light,
Where the saints, all immortal and fair,
Are robed in their garments of white.

CHO.—Over there, over there,
Oh, think of the home over there,
Over there, over there, over there,
Oh, think of the friends over there.

2 Oh, think of the friends over there,
Who before us the journey have trod,
Of the songs that they breathe on the air,
In their home in the palace of God.

3 My Saviour is now over there,
There my kindred and friends are at rest;
Then away from my sorrow and care,
Let me fly to the land of the blest.

JESUS SAVES ME ALL THE TIME. 103.

JAS. NICHOLSON.   J. A. DUNCAN.

1. Je - sus saves me eve - ry day, Je - sus saves me eve - ry night;
2. Je - sus saves when I re - pine, Je - sus saves when I re - joice;

Je - sus saves me all the way—Thro' the dark-ness, thro' the light;
Je - sus saves when hopes de-cline—Faith can al - ways hear His voice;

Je - sus saves, O bliss sub-lime—Je - sus saves me all the time.
Je - sus saves, O bliss sub-lime—Je - sus saves me all the time.

3 Jesus saves me, He is mine;
 Jesus saves me, I am His;
 Jesus saves while I recline—
 On His precious promises.

4 Jesus saves, He saves from sin,
 Jesus saves, I feel Him nigh;
 Jesus saves, He dwells within,
 Gladly do I testify.

I AM JESUS' LITTLE LAMB. 104.

Words and Music by R. E. HUDSON.

1. Je - sus bids the children come, Lov-ing Him, trust-ing Him;
2. We are safe in Je - sus' arms, Lov-ing Him, trust-ing Him;
3. If we love Him here be - low, Fol-low Him! fol-low Him!
CHO.— I am Je - sus' lit - tle Lamb, Lov-ing Him, trust-ing Him;

Je - sus bids the chil - dren come, Come with-out de - lay.
He will keep us from all harm, If we do not stray.
Home to heav-en we shall go, Hap-py with the Lord.
I am Je - sus' lit - tle Lamb, Hap-py all the day.

105. SUFFER THE CHILDREN TO COME.

L. H. B.

L. H. BAKER.

Duett.

1. "Suf-fer the children to come un-to Me, For-bid them not, for-
2. Je-sus shall gath-er the lambs with His arms, And car-ry them, and
3. Shepherd so ten-der, so lov-ing and strong, I come to Thee, I

bid them not," For of such is the king-dom of
car - ry them, Safe-ly held in His bo - som, and
come to Thee To be kept by Thy pow - er, and

heav-en," said He, For - bid them not, for - bid them not.
free from all harm, He'll car - ry them, He'll car - ry them.
saved from the wrong, I come to Thee, I come to Thee.

CHORUS.

I am so glad that Je-sus said: "Suf-fer the children to come (un-to Me);"

I am so glad that Je-sus said: "Of such is the kingdom of heaven."

Copyrighted, 1885, by R. E. HUDSON.

106. CONTENTMENT.

1 His name yields the richest perfume,
  And sweeter than music His voice;
His presence disperses my gloom,
  And makes all within me rejoice;
I should, were He always thus nigh,
  Have nothing to wish or to fear;
No mortal so happy as I,—
  My Summer would last all the year:

2 Content with beholding His face,
  My all to His pleasure resigned,
No changes of season nor place
  Would make any change in my mind:
While blest with a sense of His love,
  A palace a toy would appear;
And prisons would palaces prove,
  If Jesus would dwell with me there.

JESUS IS CALLING. 107.

Words and Music by R. E. Hudson.

CHORUS.

1. { Come, ye weary and oppressed, Jesus now is calling you,
     Come to him, he'll give you rest, (OMIT) . . . Still he bids you come.
2. { Tho' your sins like mountains rise, Jesus now is calling you,
     He has made the sacrifice, (OMIT) . . . Still he bids you come.

Jesus now is calling, calling, calling, Jesus now is calling you, calling you to come.
calling, calling, calling, calling, calling, calling,

3 Though your sins like scarlet be,
Jesus now is calling you,
From your sins he'll set you free,
Still he bids you come.

4 Come, ye wand'rers from the fold,
Jesus now is calling you,
Oh, his love can ne'er be told,
Still he bids you come.

LOOK TO JESUS. 108.

Words and Music by R. E. Hudson.

1. Look to Je - sus, look to Je - sus, Look, look, to - day,
2. Look to Je - sus, look to Je - sus, Look, look, to - day,
3. Look to Je - sus, look to Je - sus, Look, look, to - day,

When you're tempted, look to Je - sus, He'll ne'er turn a - way.
When in trou - ble, look to Je - sus, He'll ne'er turn a - way.
When af - flict - ed he will help us, He'll ne'er turn a - way.

4 Look to Jesus, look to Jesus,
Look, look, to-day,
When in sickness, oh, how precious,
He'll ne'er turn away.

5 Look to Jesus, look to Jesus,
Look, look, to-day,
When I'm dying, he'll be near me,
He'll ne'er turn away.

GIVE ME PEACE.

Rev. Frank Pollock.   Chas. Edw. Pollock.

1. From all of guilt and anxious fear, Dear Saviour, set me free; O
2. No oth-er rest-ing place I find, From sense of want and care, Than
3. Smile on my brok-en, long-ing heart, Up-lift-ed for thy light; O

keep my heart in per-fect peace, My mind is stayed on thee.
thy great strength that qui-ets me, Thro' earn-est, trust-ing prayer.
keep my soul in per-fect peace, Till faith is lost in sight.

CHORUS.

Per-fect peace, sweet peace; Per-fect peace, sweet peace;
Perfect peace, sweet peace; Perfect peace, sweet

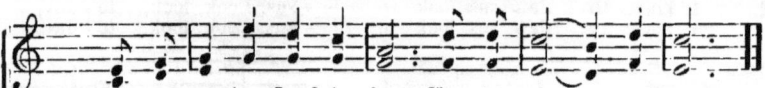

peace; I am trusting, Lord, in thee! Keep in peace, sweet peace.

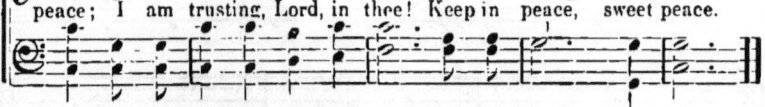

110.   A HEART OF PRAISE.

1 O for a heart to praise my God,
   A heart from sin set free;
   A heart that always feels thy blood,
   So freely shed for me.

2 A heart resigned, submissive, meek,
   My great Redeemer's throne;
   Where only Christ is heard to speak,
   Where Jesus reigns alone.

3 A heart in every thought renewed,
   And full of love divine;
   Perfect, and right, and pure, and good,
   A copy, Lord, of thine.

4 Thy nature, gracious Lord, impart;
   Come quickly from above;
   Write thy new name upon my heart,
   Thy new, best name of love.

JESUS IS MINE.

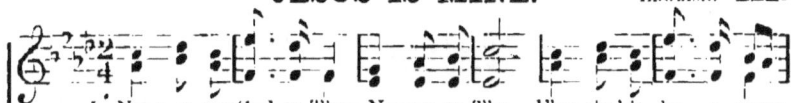

1. Near-er, my God, to Thee, Near-er to Thee, E'en tho' it be a cross,
2. Tho' like a wan-der-er, Daylight all gone, Darkness be o-ver me,
3. There let the way appear Steps up to heaven; All that thou sendest me,

That raiseth me; Still all my song shall be, Near-er, my God, to Thee!
My rest a stone; Yet in my dreams I'd be, Nearer, my God, to Thee!
In mer-cy given; An-gels to beck-on me Near-er, my God, to Thee!

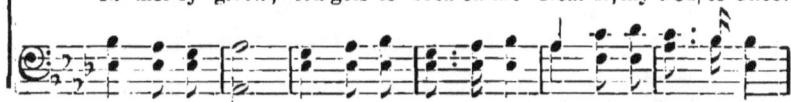

Near-er, my God, to Thee! Nearer to Thee! I will be Thine!
Near-er, my God, to Thee! Nearer to Thee! (2d-Je-sus is mine!
Near-er, my God, to Thee! Nearer to Thee!

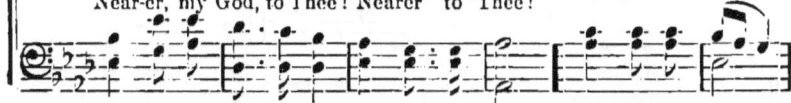

I will be Thine! Je-sus, my Sav-iour King! I will be Thine!
Je-sus is mine! Je-sus, has sat-is-fied! Je-sus is mine!

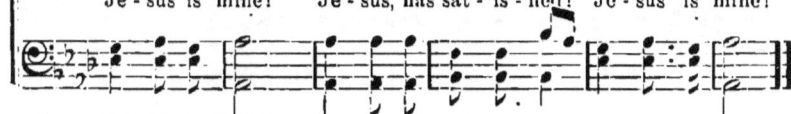

Copyrighted, 1885, by R. E. HUDSON.

Tune.—ST. THOMAS. 112.

1 I love thy church, O God!
Her walls before thee stand,
Dear as the apple of thine eye,
And graven on thy hand.

2 For her my tears shall fall;
For her my prayers ascend;
To her my cares and toils be given.
Till toils and cares shall end.

3 Beyond my highest joy,
I prize her heavenly ways;
Her sweet communion, solemn vows,
Her hymns of love and praise.

4 Sure as thy truth shall last,
To Zion shall be given
The brightest glories earth can yield,
And brighter bliss of heaven.

113. JESUS, LEAD THE WAY.

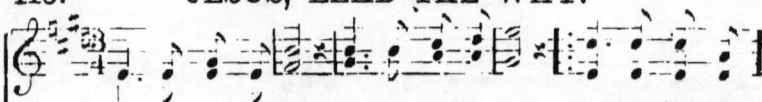

1. Je - sus, lead the way, So we shall not stray { From the path while here a - bid - ing, / But shall fol - low thy safe guid-ing; { Lead us by the hand, To that bet - ter land.

2. Should our fare be hard, Be thou our re-ward; { Should our days be ve - ry drea - ry, / And our burd-ens ve - ry wea - ry, { Lead us by the hand, To that bet - ter land.

3. Should the tempter's darts Vex and wound our hearts, { Then in all our woe and weak-ness, / Grant us pa-tience, grant us meekn-ess; { Lead us by the hand, To that bet - ter land.

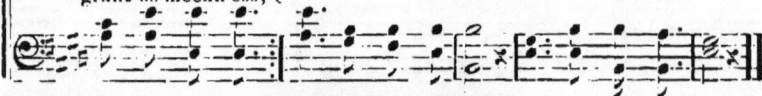

Rit.   *Rall.*

114. SILENT NIGHT.

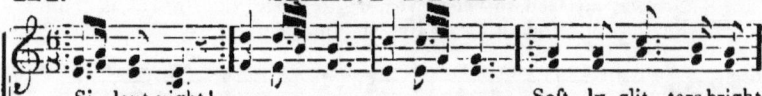

1. Si - lent night! hallowed night! Land and deep si - lent sleep, Soft - ly glit - ters bright Beck - on - ing Is - ra -

Beth - le-hem's star, el's eye from afar, Where the Saviour is born, Where the Saviour is born.

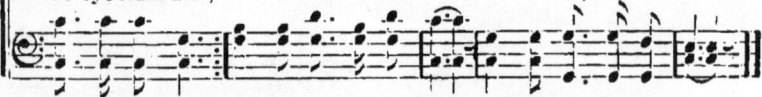

2 Silent night! hallowed night!
On the plain wakes the strain.
Sung by heavenly harbingers bright,
Filled with tidings of boundless delight,
‖: Jesus, the Saviour, has come:‖

3 Silent night! hallowed night!
Earth, awake! silence break!
High your chorus of melody raise,
Sing to heaven in anthems of praise,
‖: Peace forever shall reign.:‖

WHY WILL YE DIE? 115.

Words and Music by H. H. H.

1. Sin-ner, for thee, A par-don so free, Though dark thy ca-
2. Tired of thy sin And sor-row with-in, Thy soul longs to
3. Death is at hand Thy life to de-mand: Make haste, now, thy

reer may have been, That bur-den shall roll From thy guil-ty
find its true joy— The joy that thy King In mer-cy doth
Sav-iour to find; No long-er de-lay, You're pass-ing a-

CHORUS.

soul When the light of His face thou hast seen. Why wilt thou die?
bring, Thy sor-row and sin to de-stroy.
way, And Sa-tan your soul waits to bind.

| 1st. | 2d. |

Why wilt thou die? Sin-ner, sin-ner, why? why?

Music No. 20 Gems of Gospel Song. 116.

1 Come, weary sinner, to the Cross;
  The Saviour bids you come;
  Come, trusting in his precious blood;
  Wait not—there still is room.

CHO.—Jesus now is passing by,
  Passing by, passing by,
  Jesus now is passing by,
  I'll go out to meet him.

While he is so very nigh,
  Very nigh, very nigh,
  While he is so very nigh,
  I'll go out and greet him.

2 He waits to fill your soul with joy,
  And all your sins forgive;
  His love for you no tongue can tell;
  Oh! trust his grace and live!

MY DREAM.

Words and Music by R. E. Hudson.

1. I had a dream of long a - go, I heard them sing once more,
2. Now while they sang, poor sin-ners came With tears of sor-row cried:
3. Then each with joy be-gan to tell, Of Je - sus and his love,

SING ONE VERSE OF NO. 118 AS FIRST CHORUS.

The same old songs they used to sing In long gone days of yore.
What shall I do? I heard them say, Look to the cru-ci-fied,
While old and young in repturous strain Would sing of joys a-bove,

SING ONE VERSE OF NO. 119 AS SECOND CHORUS.

They sang of Him, who died for me,—How sweet it was to hear
Then while they prayed in Je - sus' name, That they might now be-lieve;
Now as the part - ing hour had come, When they must say good-by

SING ONE VERSE OF NO. 120 AS THIRD CHORUS.

The old, old hymn my moth-er sang, In ac - cent soft and clear.
I heard a shout that thrilled my soul, I do my Lord re - ceive.
They joined in ayer then sang once more I'll to thy bos - som fly.

1. A - las! and did my Sav-iour bleed? And did my Sovereign die?
2. Was it for crimes that I have done, He groaned up-on the tree?
3. But drops of grief can ne'er re - pay The debt of love I owe;

Would he de - vote that sac - red head For such a worm as I?
A - maz - ing pi - ty! grace un-known! And love be-yond de-gree!
Here, Lord, I give my - self to thee, 'Tis all that I can do.

:S: CHOSUS.

1. { O hap - py day, that fixed my choice On thee, my Sav - iour, and my God!
     Well may this glow-ing heart re - joice, And tell its rapt - ures all a - broad. } Hap-py

Fine.   D. S.

day, hap - py day, When Je-sus wash'd my sins a - way! { He taught me how to watch and pray,
                                                            And live re - joic - ing ev-ery day; }

2. 'Tis done, the great transaction's done,
   I am my Lord's and he is mine;
   He drew me, and I followed on.
   Charmed to confess the voice divine.

3. Now rest, my long divided heart:
   Fixed on this blissful centre, rest;
   Nor ever from thy Lord depart,
   With him of every good possessed.

MARTYN.

S. B. Marsh.   *Fine.*

1. { Je-sus, lov-er of my soul, Let me to thy bos-om fly, }
   { While the bil-lows near me roll, While the temp-est still is high; }
D. C. Safe in-to the ha-ven guide, O re-ceive my soul at last.

2. { Oth-er ref-uge have I none; Hangs my help-less soul on thee; }
   { Leave, O leave me not a-lone; Still sup-port and com-fort me: }
D. C. Cov-er my de-fence-less head With the sha-dow of thy wing.

D. C.

Hide me, O my Sav-iour, hide,   Till the storm of life is past;
All my trust on thee is stayed;   All my help for thee I bring;

3. Thou, O Christ, art all I want: Just and holy is thy name;
   More than all in thee I find: I am all unrighteousness;
   Raise the fallen, cheer the faint,   False, and full of sin I am;
   Heal the sick and lead the blind.   Thou art full of truth and grace.

121.   **DEPTH OF MERCY.**

REV. CHAS. WESLEY.   J. STEVENSON.

1. { Depth of mer-cy, can there be   Mer-cy Still re-served for me? }
   { Can my God his wrath for-bear? Me, the thief of sin-ners spare? }

2. { I have long withstood his grace, Long pro-voked him to his face; }
   { Would not hearken to his calls, Grieved him by a thou-sand falls. }

3. { Now in-cline me to re-pent, Let me now my sins la-ment; }
   { Now my foul re-volt de-plore, Weep, be-lieve, and sin no more. }

CHORUS.   *Smoothly.*   *Repeat pp*

{ God is love, I do be-lieve; }
{ He is wait-ing to for-give, }   He is wait-ing, wait-ing to for-give.

SATISFIED.

Miss Clara Teale.　　　Psalms 36 : 8.　　　R. E. Hudson.

1. All my life long I had pant- ed For a draught from some cool
2. Feed-ing on the husks around me, Till my strength was almost
3. Poor I was, and sought for rich - es, Something that would satis-
4. Well of wa - ter, ev - er springing, Bread of life so rich and

spring, That I hoped would quench the burning Of the thirst I felt with-in.
gone. Longed my soul for something better, Only still to hun-ger on.
fy, But the dust I gathered round me Only mocked my soul's sad cry.
free, Untold wealth that never faileth, My Redeem-er is to me.

CHORUS.

Hal-le - lu - jah! I have found him—Whom my soul so long has

craved! Je-sus sat - isfies my longings; Thro' his blood I now am saved.

1 Come, thou Fount of every blessing,
　Tune my heart to sing thy grace:
Streams of mercy, never ceasing,
　Call for songs of loudest praise.
Jesus sought me when a stranger,
　Wand'ring from the fold of God;
He, to rescue me from danger,
　Interposed his precious blood.

2 O! to grace how great a debtor
　Daily I'm constrain'd to be!
Let thy goodness, like a fetter,
　Bind my loving heart to thee.
Prone to love thee, Lord, I feel it—
　Prone to trust the God I love;
Here's my heart, O take and seal it;
　Seal it for thy courts above.

THEY COME.

Not to fast.

Words and Music by R. E. HUDSON.

1. A-wake, a-wake, a-wake ye sons of free-dom, hark!
2. Go forth, go forth, go forth and re-scue fal-len men:
3. We'll win, we'll win, for God is on the side of right;

A-wake, a-wake

A - wake, a - wake, a - wake, and hear their cry;
For God, and home, and free-dom's land be true;
We'll work, we'll pray, the day may quick-ly come,

A - wake, a - wake,

They come, they come and ask your help their sons to save
Gird on, gird on, the ar-mor of our fath-ers' God,
When men, when men and wo-men ov-er all our land

The come, they come,

Rit. to close.

From rum, foul rum; Oh! help us, or we die.
And stand for right, Our coun-try calls for you.
Unite to stop the Sale of poi-son-ed rum.

125. Music No. 126.

1 Long have I striven from sin to flee,
Wishing my Saviour would set me free;
When I was willing to trust, not see;
Jesus gave me rest.

CHORUS:

Jesus gave me rest, Jesus gave me rest,
Just when I trusted His power to save,
Jesus gave me rest.

2 I am so happy from day to day,
Often my path is a thorny way;
But near my Saviour's side I stay,
Jesus gives me rest.

3 Glory to Jesus! my song shall be,
Now, and all through eternity,
When I was longing to be set free,
Jesus gave me rest.

GLORY TO HIS NAME! 126.

E. A. HOFFMAN.   Ps. 63 : 4   REV. J. H. STOCKTON, by per.

1. Down at the cross where the Saviour died, Down where for cleansing from sin I cried,
2. I am so wondrously saved from sin; Je-sus so sweetly abides within,
3. Come to this fountain, so rich and sweet; Humble your soul at the Saviour's feet;

Fine.

There to my heart was the blood ap-plied, Glo-ry to his name!
Saves me each moment, and keeps me clean; Glo-ry to his name!
Plunge in to-day, and be made complete, Glo-ry to his name!

D.S Now to my heart is the blood ap-plied, Glo-ry to his name!

CHORUS.   **D.S.**

Glo-ry to his name!   Glo-ry to his name!

I'LL LIVE FOR HIM. 127.

C. R. DUNBAR.

1. My life, my love I give to thee, Thou Lamb of God, who died for me; Oh,

CHO.—I'll live for Him who died for me, How hap-py then my life shall be! I'll

may I ev-er faith-ful be, My Sa-vior and my God!

live for Him who died for me, My Sa-vior and my God.

2. I now believe thou dost receive,
For thou hast died that I might live;
And now henceforth I'll trust in thee,
My Savior and my God!

3. Oh, thou who died on Calvary,
To save my soul and make me free,
I consecrate my life to thee,
My Savior and my God!

128. THE HALF HAS NEVER BEEN TOLD

FRANCES RIDLEY HAVERGAL.   1 Cor. 2:9.   R. E. HUDSON.

1. I know I love thee bet-ter, Lord, Than an-y earth-ly joy, For
2. I know that thou art near-er still Than an-y earthly throng, And
3. Thou hast put gladness in my heart; Then well may I be glad! With
4. O Saviour, pre-cious Saviour mine! What will thy presence be If

thou hast giv-en me the peace Which noth-ing can de-stroy.
sweet-er is the thought of thee Than an-y love-ly song.
out the se-cret of thy love I could not but be sad.
such a life of joy can crown Our walk on earth with thee?

CHORUS.

The half has never yet been told,   Of love so full and free;
    yet been told,

Rit.

The half has never yet been told,   The blood—it cleanseth me.
    yet been told,   cleanseth me

129.

1 Plunged in a gulf of dark despair,
  We wretched sinners lay,
  Without one cheering beam of hope,
  Or spark of glimm'ring day.

2 With pitying eyes the Prince of peace
  Beheld our helpless grief:
  He saw, and (O amazing love!)
  He flew to our relief.

3 Down from the shining seats above,
  With joyful haste he fled;
  Enter'd the grave in mortal flesh,
  And dwelt among the dead.

4 O for this love, let rocks and hills
  Their lasting silence break;
  And all harmonious human tongues
  The Savior's praises speak.

Affettuoso.

1. When shall we meet a - gain, Meet ne'er to sev - er? When will peace
2. When shall love free - ly flow, Pure as life's riv - er? When shall sweet
3. Up to that world of light Take us, dear Saviour; May we all

wreathe her chain Round us for - ev - er? Our hearts will ne'er re-pose Safe
friendship glow, Changeless for-ev - er? Where joys ce - les-tial thrill, Where
there u - nite, Hap - py for - ev - er? Where kindred spir-its dwell, There

from each blast that blows In this dark vale of woe, Nev-er, no, nev-er.
bliss each heart shall fill, And fears of parting chill Nev-er, no, nev-er!
may our music swell, And time our joys dis-pell, Nev-er, no, nev-er!

131.   Air—"SWEET BY-AND-BY."   132.

1 We've a band that shall conquer the foe,
  If we fight in the strength of the King;
  With the sword of the Spirit we know
  We shall sinners to Calvary bring.

Cho.—I believe we shall win,
  If we fight in the strength of the King;
  I believe we shall win,
  If we fight in the strength of the King.

2 We have conquered in times that are past,
  And we've scattered the foe from the field;
  Then we'll fight for the King till the last,
  And the sword of the Spirit we'll wield.

3 Our foe may be mighty and brave,
  And the fighting be hard and severe,
  But the King is the mighty to save,
  And in conflict He always is near.

4 In the name of the King we will fight,
  With our banners unfurled to the breeze;
  We will battle for God and the right,
  And the kingdom of Satan we'll seize.

1 We will hope, we will trust in the Lord,
  He is faithful and true to the end;
  We can always rely on His word,
  And in Him can confide as a friend.

Cho.—In the home of the blest,
  All our labor and toil will be o'er;
  Safe at home we shall rest
  From our labor and toil evermore.

2 Let us follow the Saviour of love,
  For the burden is easy and light;
  And the mansions are ready above,
  In the land of eternal delight.

3 In that beautiful home of the blest
  There's no sickness or sorrow of heart;
  There the weary forever shall rest
  And the faithful receive their reward.

4 We will wait, we will labor and pray,
  We will watch, tho' the night seemeth long,
  For we soon shall enjoy the bright day,
  And will join in the beautiful song.

133. SIMPLY TRUSTING EVERY DAY.

EDGAR PAGE. Psalms 125 : 1. R. E. HUDSON.

1. Sim-ply trust-ing ev-ery day, Trusting thro' a storm-y
2. Bright-ly doth his Spir-it shine In-to this poor heart of
3. Sing-ing, if my way is clear, Pray-ing, if the path is

way; Ev-en when my faith is small, Trusting Je-sus, that is all.
mine; While he leads I can-not fall, Trusting Je-sus, that is all.
drear; If in dan-ger, for him call; Trusting Je-sus, that is all.

Till within the jas-per wall, Trusting Je-sus, that is all.

CHORUS. D.S.

Trusting him while life shall last, Trusting him till earth is past;

134. WE WILL HAVE A HAPPY TIME?

Words and Music by R. E. HUDSON.

1. Parents, wont you come along? Parents, won't you come along?
2. There we'll sit at Je-sus' feet, There we'll sit at Je-sus' feet,

CHO. *There we'll have a hap-py time, There we'll have a happy time, &c.*

Parents, won't you come a-long To the New Je-ru-sa-lem?
There we'll sit at Je-sus' feet, In the New Je-ru-sa-lem.

3. Children, won't you go along? &c.   4. There we shall our loved ones meet &c.

Mrs. M. B. C. Slade.   Dr. A. B. Everett.

1. If I, like Gal - i - lee fish-ers, Were mending my nets by the main,
2. If I were dwelling in pleasure, Or sit - ting in plac - es of gain,
3. If I were sink-ing in sad-ness, Or dreading the cross and the pain,

And Je - sus, com-ing, should call me.)
And Je - sus, pass-ing, should call me. } He nev - er should call in vain.
And Je - sus ten - der - ly call'd me.)

CHORUS.

Then fol - low the summons of Je - sus, Where-ev-er, how-ev er it falls;

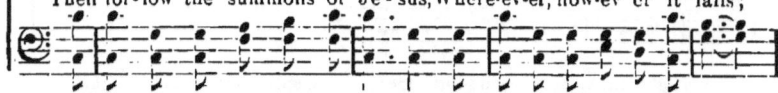

For high up the pathway He sees us, And, "Follow thou me!" He calls.

By per. of R. M. McIntosh.

CRIMSON WAVE. 136.

1 O, now I see the crimson wave,
  The fountain deep and wide;
Jesus, my Lord, mighty to save,
  Points to his wounded side.

Cho.--The cleansing stream, I see, I see!
  I plunge, and O it cleanseth me :
O, praise the Lord, it cleanseth me!
  It cleanseth me, yes, cleanseth me.

2 I see the new creation rise,
  I hear the speaking blood :
It speaks! polluted nature dies !
  Sinks 'neath the cleansing flood.

3 I rise to walk in heaven's own light,
  Above the world and sin,
With heart made pure, and garments white
  And Christ enthroned within.

137. BE GUIDING ME.

Words and Music by Mrs. T. M. GRIFFIN, by per.

Slowly.

1. When my way is bright as morning, And my heart from care is free, Be Thy
2. When my heart is almost yielding To the pow'rs that e-vil be, Let Thy
3. When my days are long and weary, And my soul a ray would see 'Mid the
4. When my walk thro' life is o-ver, And my spir-it flies to Thee, May it

grace my life a-dorn-ing, And Thy light be guid-ing me.
love my soul be shield-ing, And Thy light be guid-ing me.
storm-clouds, dark and drear-y, Let Thy light be guid-ing me.
then in joy dis-cov-er How Thy light was guid-ing me.

CHORUS.

Guid-ing me,.......... O bless-ed Sav-iour, Let Thy

Ev-en me, O bless-ed Saviour, ev-en me,

light......... be guid-ing me; Guiding me,......... guid-ing

Let Thy light be guid-ing me; Ev-en me,

me,........ Let Thy light............ be guid-ing me.

ev-en me, Let Thy light be guid - ing me, ev-en me.

Arranged by R. E. Hudson.

1. Love, freedom, peace. and ceaseless blessing, All, all for thee,
2. Peace, flow-ing calm-ly as a riv-er, Now you may find;
3. Joy, dear-er than a thousand treasures, Wilt thou re-ceive;

If, while your sin-ful-ness confessing, To your Redeemer you flee.
From all your sor-row He'll de-liv-er While to his will you're resigned.
Jes-us will give it without measure If you will on-ly be-lieve.

CHORUS.

All the world can ne'er give com-fort, Can-not give thee joy,

Je-sus a-lone can sat-is-fy thee, He will thy sor-row destroy.

Music 155 Gems and Echoes Combined. 139.

1. Christ has for sin atonement made—
   What a wonderful Saviour!
   We are redeemed! the price is paid!
   What a wonderful Saviour!

Cho.—What a wonderful Saviour
   Is Jesus, my Jesus!
   What a wonderful Saviour
   Is Jesus, my Lord!

2. He cleansed my heart from all its sin,
   What a wonderful Saviour!
   And now he reigns and rules therein;
   What a wonderful Saviour!

3. To him I've given all my heart,
   What a wonderful Saviour!
   The world shall never share a part;
   What a wonderful Saviour!

HOMEWARD BOUND.

R. E. Hudson.   Arranged by R. E. Hudson.

1. { We are out up-on the o-cean, bound for home, Where the
   { And my soul is filled with rap-ture on the way, For we

2. { He has land-ed man-y pil grims safe-ly home, Where no
   { There we'll meet with all our loved ones gone be-fore, And we'll

3. { Come and go with us to-day, we'll soon be home; While the
   { Je - sus waits to save you now from all your sin, Will you

winds and waves of sor-row nev-er come;
soon shall reach the land of end-less day. }   We are homeward bound for
sin with all its sorrows ne'er can come; }
tell His woudrous love for-ev-er-more. }
Spir-it now in-vites you, sin-ner, come! }
o-pen now your heart and let Him in. }

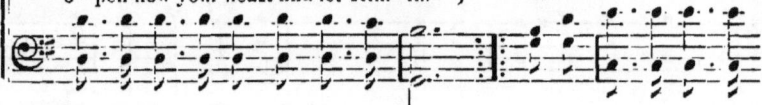

CHORUS.

glo-ry,   Homeward bound for glo-ry!   There we'll meet with

Yes, we're homeward bound for glo-ry, There we'll meet with all our

loved ones gone be-fore;   We are homeward bound for glory,

loved ones gone be-fore;   We are homeward bound for glo-ry, Yes, we're

HOMEWARD BOUND.—Concluded.

Homeward bound for glo-ry !   All the storms of life will soon be o'er.

homeward bound, O hal-le- lu-jah !

HE IS MINE.   141.

J. W. McABEE.

1. The Saviour is mine, His power divine, Has set my soul free, And His I will be ;
   [From
2. The pure crystal sea, The life giving tree, His glory, His grace, His loving embrace,
   [All
3. The King on His throne Is mine, all my own; The joy of this hour, The conquer-
   [ing power, He's

guilt I was sad, And He made me glad, I'll praise Him again, Oh, glory ! amen.
that He has made, The sunshine, the shade, He's written this line, All, all things are
   [thine.
mine, all His love, His glo-ry a-bove, His radiant throne, All, all are my own.

CHORUS.

He is mine, He is mine, I know He is mine, He is mine, He is mine, I know He is
   [mine.

Is He thine? Is He thine? Do you know He is thine? Is He thine? Is He thine?
   [Do you know He is thine?

142. GLORIOUS FOUNTAIN.

COWPER.   T. C. O'KANE.

1. { There is a foun-tain filled with blood, filled with blood,
And sin-ners plunged beneath that blood, beneath that blood, be-

2. { The dy-ing thief re-joiced to see, rejoiced to see, re-
And there may I, tho' vile as he, tho' vile as he, tho'

filled with blood, There is a foun-tain filled with blood, Drawn
neath that flood, And sin-ners plunged be-neath that flood, Lose
joiced to see, The dy-ing thief re-joiced to see, That
vile as he, And there may I, tho' vile as he, Wash

CHORUS.

from Immanuel's veins, }
all their guil-ty stains, }
foun-tain in his day, }
all my sins a-way. }
     Oh come to this fountain, Come, come to-

day And trust-ing Je-sus, Wash your sins a-way.

3. Thou dying Lamb, ‖: thy precious blood,:‖
Thou dying Lamb, thy precious blood
Shall never lose its power,
Till all the ransomed ‖: Church of God,:‖
Till all the ransomed Church of God
Are saved, to sin no more.

4. E'er since by faith ‖: I saw the stream,:‖
E'er since by faith I saw the stream
Thy flowing wounds supply,
Redeeming love ‖: has been my theme,:‖
Redeeming love has been my theme,
And shall be till I die.

143   Tune, Lenox.

1 Blow ye the trumpet, blow,
  The gladly solemn sound;
Let all the nations know,
  To earth's remotest bound,
The year of jubilee is come ;
Return, ye ransomed sinners, home,

2 Jesus, our great High Priest,
  Hath full atonement made ;
Ye weary spirits, rest ;
  Ye mournful souls, be glad ;
The year of jubilee is come ;
Return, ye ransomed sinners, home.

3 Extol the Lamb of God,—
  The all-atoning Lamb ;
Redemption in his blood
  Throughout the world proclaim ;
The year of jubilee is come ;
Return, ye ransomed sinners, home.

144   Tune, Nettleton.

- Hark ! the voice of Jesus calling,
  Who will go and work to-day ?
Fields are white, the harvest waiting,
  Who will bear the sheaves away ?
Loud and long the Master calleth,
  Rich reward he offers free;
Who will answer, gladly saying,
  "Here am I, O Lord, send me."

2 While the souls of men are dying,
  And the Master calls for you,
Let none hear you idly saying,
  "There is nothing I can do!"
Gladly take the task he gives you,
  Let his work your pleasure be;
Answer quickly when he calleth,
  "Here am I, O Lord, send me."

145   Tune, Nettleton.

Jesus, I my cross have taken,
  All to leave and follow thee ;
Naked, poor, despised, forsaken,
  Thou from hence my all shalt be.
Perish every fond ambition,
  All I've sought, or hoped, or known ;
Yet how rich is my condition !
  God and heaven are still my own.

Let the world despise and leave me,
  They have left my Savior, too ;
Human hearts and looks deceive me—
  Thou art not, like them, untrue.
And while thou shalt smile upon me,
  God of wisdom, love and might,
Foes may hate and friends may shun me,
  Show thy face and all is bright.

146   Tune, Zion.

1 Zion stands with hills surrounded,
  Zion, kept by power divine.
All her foes shall be confounded,
  Though the world in arms combine ;
    Happy Zion—
  What a favored lot is thine !

2 Every human tie may perish ;
  Friend to friend unfaithful prove ;
Mothers cease their own to cherish ;
  Heaven and earth at last remove ;
    But no changes
  Can attend Jehovah's love.

3 In the furnace God may prove thee,
  Thence to bring thee forth more bright
But can never cease to love thee ;
  Thou art precious in his sight ;
    God is with thee—
  God, thine everlasting light.

147   Tune, How Can I Keep From Singing ?

My life flows on in endless song ;
  Above earth's lamentation,
I catch the sweet, though far off hymn,
  That hails a new creation ;
Thro' all the tumult and the strife,
  I hear the music ringing;
It finds an echo in my soul—
  How can I keep from singing ?

What tho' my joys and comforts die ?
  The Lord my Savior liveth ;
What tho' the darkness gather round ?
  Songs in the night he giveth ;
No storm can shake my inmost calm,
  While to that refuge clinging ;
Since Christ is Lord of heaven and earth,
  How can I keep from singing ?

148   Tune, Webb.

1 Stand up ! stand up for Jesus !
  Ye soldiers of the cross ;
Lift high his royal banner,
  It must not suffer loss ;
From victory unto victory
  His army he shall lead,
Till every foe is vanquished,
  And Christ is Lord indeed.

2 Stand up ! stand up for Jesus !
  Stand in his strength alone ;
The arm of flesh will fail you—
  Ye dare not trust your own ;
Put on the Gospel armor,
  And, watching unto prayer,
Where duty calls, or danger,
  Be never wanting there.

149   Tune, Windham.

1 Show pity, Lord, O Lord, forgive;
   Let a repenting rebel live.
   Are not thy mercies large and free?
   May not a sinner trust in thee?

2 My crimes are great, but don't surpass
   The power and glory of thy grace;
   Great God, thy nature hath no bound—
   So let thy pard'ning love be found.

3 O wash my soul from every sin;
   And make my guilty conscience clean;
   Here on my heart the burden lies,
   And past offenses pain my eyes.

4 My lips with shame my sins confess,
   Against thy law, against thy grace;
   Lord, should thy judgment grow severe
   I am condemned, but thou art clear.

150   Tune, Coronation.

1 All hail the power of Jesus' name!
   Let angels prostrate fall;
   Bring forth the royal diadem,
   And crown him lord of all.

2 Sinners, whose love can ne'er forget
   The wormwood and the gall,
   Go, spread your trophies at his feet,
   And crown him Lord of all.

3 Let every kindred, every tribe,
   On this terrestrial ball,
   To him all majesty ascribe,
   And crown him Lord of all.

4 Oh! that with yonder sacred throng
   We at his feet may fall;
   We'll join the everlasting song,
   And crown him Lord of all.

151   Tune, Pisgah.

1 When I can read my title clear
   To mansions in the skies,
   I'll bid farewell to every fear,
   And wipe my weeping eyes.

2 Should earth against my soul engage
   And fiery darts be hurled,
   Then I can smile at Satan's rage,
   And face a frowning world.

3 Let cares like a wild deluge come,
   Let storms of sorrow fall,
   So I but safely reach my home,
   My God, my heaven, my all.

4 There I shall bathe my weary soul
   In seas of heavenly rest,
   And not a wave of trouble roll
   Across my peaceful breast.

152   Tune, Dennis.

1 Blest be the tie that binds
   Our hearts in Christian love;
   The fellowship of kindred minds
   Is like to that above.

2 Before our Father's throne
   We pour our ardent prayers;
   Our fears, our hopes, our aims are one—
   Our comforts and our cares.

3 We share our mutual woes,
   Our mutual burdens bear,
   And often for each other flows
   The sympathetic tear.

4 When we asunder part,
   It gives us inward pain,
   But we shall still be joined in heart,
   And hope to meet again.

153   Tune, Woodstock.

Just as I am—without one plea,
But that thy blood was shed for me,
And that thou bidst me come to thee.
   O Lamb of God, I come.

Just as I am—and waiting not,
To rid my soul of one dark spot—
To thee whose blood can cleanse each blot
   O Lamb of God I come.

Just as I am—thou wilt receive,
Wilt welcome, pardon, cleanse, relieve,
Because thy promise I believe.
   O Lamb of God, I come.

Just as I am—thy love, I own,
Has broken every barrier down;
Now to be thine, yea, thine alone,
   O Lamb of God, I come.

154   Tune, Nettleton.

1 Love divine, all love excelling,
   Joy of heaven, to earth come down,
   Fix in us thy humble dwelling;
   All thy faithful mercies crown.
   Jesus, thou art all compassion—
   Pure, unbounded love thou art;
   Visit us with thy salvation;
   Enter every trembling heart.

2 Breathe, oh breathe thy loving Spirit
   Into every troubled breast!
   Let us all in thee inherit,
   Let us find that second rest.
   Take away our bent to sinning;
   Alpha and Omega be;
   End of faith, as its beginning,
   Set our hearts at liberty.

155 Tune, Lenox.

1 Arise, my soul, arise,
   Shake off thy guilty fears;
The bleeding sacrifice
   In my behalf appears;
Before the throne my Surety stands,
My name is written on his hands.

2 Five bleeding wounds he bears,
   Received on Calvary;
They pour effectual prayer,
   They strongly plead for me;
Forgive him, O forgive. they cry,
Nor let that ransomed sinner die.

3 My God is reconciled,
   His pardoning voice I hear;
He owns me for his child;
   I can no longer fear:
With confidence I now draw nigh,
And Father, Abba Father, cry.

156 Tune, Out on the Ocean Sailing.

1 We are out on the ocean sailing,
   Homeward bound we sweetly glide;
We are out on the ocean sailing
To our home beyond the tide.

CHORUS.
All the storms will soon be over,
   Then we'll anchor in the harbor;
We are out on the ocean sailing
To our home beyond the tide.

2 Millions now are safely landed
   Over on the golden shore;
Millions more are on their journey,
Yet there's room for millions more.

3 Come on board and ship for glory,
   Be in haste, make up your mind,
For our vessel's weighing anchor,
Or you'll soon be left behind.

157 Tune, My All Is on the Altar.

1 My body, soul and spirit,
   Jesus, I give to thee,
A consecrated off'ring,
   Thine evermore to be.

CHORUS.
My all is on the altar,
   I'm waiting for the fire,
Waiting, waiting, waiting,
   I'm waiting for the fire.

2 O Jesus, mighty Savior,
   I trust in thy great name,
I look for thy salvation,
   Thy promise now I claim.

3 Oh, let the fire descending
   Just now upon my soul,
Consume my humble off'ring,
And cleanse and make me whole·

158 Tune, Toplady.

1 Rock of ages, cleft for me,
Let me hide myself in thee;
Let the water and the blood,
From thy wounded side which flow'd,
Be of sin the double cure—
Save from wrath and make me pure.

2 Could my tears forever flow,
Could my zeal no languor know,
These for sin could not atone;
Thou must save and Thou alone;
In my hand no price I bring.
Simply to the cross I cling.

3 While I draw this fleeting breath,
When my eyes shall close in death,
When I rise to worlds unknown,
And behold thee on thy throne,
Rock of ages, cleft for me,
Let me hide myself in thee.

159 Tune, Every Day and Hour.

1 Savior, more than life to me,
I am clinging, clinging close to thee;
Let thy precious blood applied,
Keep me ever, ever near thy side.

CHORUS.
Every day, every hour,
Let me feel thy cleansing power;
May thy tender love to me,
Bind me closer, closer, Lord, to thee.

2 Through this changing world below
Lead me gently, gently as I go;
Trusting thee, I cannot stray,
I can never, never lose my way.

3 Let me love thee more and more,
Till this fleeting, fleeting life is o'er;
Till my soul is lost in love,
In a brighter, brighter world above.

160 Tune, I Am Trusting, Lord.

1 I am coming to the cross;
   I am poor, and weak, and blind;
I am counting all but dross,
   I shall full salvation find.

CHORUS.
I am trusting, Lord, in thee,
   Blest Lamb of Calvary;
Humbly at thy cross I bow,
   Save me, Jesus, save me now.

3 Here I give my all to thee,
   Friends, and time, and earthly store;
Soul and body, thine to be—
   Wholly thine for evermore.

4 In thy promises I trust,
   Now I feel the blood applied;
I am prostrate in the dust,
   I with Christ am crucified.

161 Music, No. 9, Gems of Gospel Song.

1 Are you weary, are you heavy-hearted?
Tell it to Jesus, tell it to Jesus.
Are you grieving over joys departed?
Tell it to Jesus alone.

CHORUS.

Tell it to Jesus, tell it to Jesus,
He is a friend well known;
You have no other such a friend or brother
Tell it to Jesus alone.

2 Do the tears flow down your cheeks
unbidden?
Tell it to Jesus, tell it to Jesus.
Have you sins that to man's eyes are
hidden?
Tell it to Jesus alone.

3 Do you fear the gath'ring clouds of
sorrow?
Tell it to Jesus, tell it to Jesus.
Are you anxious what shall be to-
morrow?
Tell it to Jesus alone.

162 Music, No. 210, Gems of Gospel Song.

1 Come ye sinners, poor and needy,
Weak and wounded, sick and sore;
Jesus ready stands to save you,
Full of pity, love and power.

CHO.—Why don't you come to Jesus?
He's waiting to receive you,
Why don't you come to
Jesus and be saved?

2 Let not conscience make you linger;
Nor of fitness fondly dream;
All the fitness he requireth
Is to feel your need of him!

3 Come ye weary heavy-laden,
Bruised and mangled by the fall;
If you tarry 'till you're better,
You will never come at all.

163 Music, No. 34, Gems of Gospel Song.

1 Take my life and let it be
Consecrated, Lord, to Thee;
Take my hands and let them move
At the impulse of thy love.

CHORUS.

Wash me in the Savior's precious blood,
Cleanse me in its purifying flood;
Lord, I give to thee my life and all to be
Thine henceforth, eternally.

2 Take my feet and let them be
Swift and beautiful to Thee;
Take my voice and let me sing
Always—only—for my King.

3 Take my will and make it thine,
It shall be no longer mine;
Take my heart, it is thine own,
It shall be thy royal throne.

164 Music, No. 226, Gems of Gospel Song.

1 What poor despised company
Of travellers are these,
That walk in yonder narrow way,
Along that rugged maze?

CHORUS.

O, I'd rather be the least of them
Who are the Lord's alone,
Than wear a royal diadem,
And sit upon a throne.

2 Ah, these are of a royal line,
All children of a King—
Heirs of immortal crowns divine,
And lo, for joy they sing.

3 Why do they then appear so mean,
And why so much despis'd?
Because of their rich robes unseen,
The world is not appris'd.

165 Music, No. 77, Gems of Gospel Song.

1 I will follow thee, my Savior,
Wheresoe'er my lot may be;
Where thou goest I will follow,
Yes, my Lord, I'll follow thee.

CHORUS.

I will follow thee, my Savior,
Thou didst shed thy blood for me;
And tho' all men should forsake thee,
By thy grace I'll follow thee.

2 Though 'tis lone, and dark, and dreary,
Cheerless though my path may be,
If thy voice I hear before me,
Fearlessly I'll follow thee.

3 Though I meet with tribulations,
Sorely tempted though I be.
I remember thou wast tempted,
And rejoice to follow thee.

166 Music, No. 199, Gems of Gospel Song

1 Now crucified with Christ I am,
The self within is slain;
But still I live, and yet not I—
Christ lives in me again.

CHORUS.

I am sinking out of self, out of self, into
Christ,
Sinking out of self into Christ,
I am sinking, sinking, sinking out of self,
Sinking out of self into Christ.

2 Dead to the world with sin I am,
Alive to God alone;
The life I have, I live by faith
In God's beloved Son.

3 Hereafter "it is no more I,"
Nor "sin" that ruleth me,
Reign, reign forever, blessed Christ,
My all I give to thee.

1 At the sounding of the trumpet, when
   the saints are gathered home,
We will greet each other by the crystal
   sea,
With the friends and all the lov'd ones
   there awaiting us to come,
What a gath'ring of the faithful that
   will be.

CHORUS.
What a gath'ring, gath'ring,
At the sounding of the glorious jubilee!
What a gath'ring, gath'ring,
What a gath'ring of the faithful that
   will be.

2 When the angel of the Lord proclaims
   that time shall be no more,
We shall gather, and the saved and
   ransomed see,
Then to meet again together, on the
   bright celestial shore,
What a gath'ring of the faithful that
   will be.

3 When the golden harps are sounding,
   and the angel bands proclaim
In triumphant strains the glorious
   jubilee,
Then to meet and join the song of
   Moses and the Lamb,
What a gath'ring of the faithful that
   will be.

168 Music, No. 11, Gems of Gospel Song.

1 Are you ready for the Bridegroom
   When he comes, when he comes?
Are you ready for the Bridegroom
   When he comes, when he comes;
Behold, he cometh! behold, he com-
   eth!
Be robed and ready, for the Bride-
   groom comes.

CHORUS
Behold the Bridegroom, for he comes,
   for he comes!
Behold the Bridegroom, for he comes,
   for he comes!
Behold, he cometh! behold, he cometh!
Be robed and ready for the Bridegroom
   comes.

2 Have your lamps trimmed and burning
   When he comes, when he comes;
Have your lamps trimmed and burning
   When he comes, when he comes;
He quickly cometh, he quickly cometh
   O soul! be ready when the Bride-
   groom comes.

I have found repose for my weary soul,
   Trusting in the promise of the Savior;
And a harbor safe when the billows roll,
   Trusting in the promise of the Savior;
I will fear no foe in the deadly strife,
   Trusting in the promise of the Savior;
I will bear my lot in the toil of life,
   Trusting in the promise of the Savior.

CHORUS.
Resting on his mighty arm forever,
Never from his loving heart to sever,
I will rest by grace in his strong embrace,
   Trusting in the promise of the Savior.

Oh, the peace and joy of the life I live,
   Trusting in the promise of the Savior;
Oh, the strength and grace only God can
   give,
   Trusting in the promise of the Savior;
Whosoever will may be saved to-day,
   Trusting in the promise of the Savior;
And begin to walk in the holy way,
   Trusting in the promise of the Savior.

170 Music, No. 17, Gems of Gospel Song

1 Sowing in the morning, sowing seeds
   of kindness,
Sowing in the noontide and the dewy
   eve;
Waiting for the harvest, and the time
   of reaping,
We shall come, rejoicing, bringing in
   the sheaves.

CHORUS.
Bringing in the sheaves, bringing in the
   sheaves,
We shall come, rejoicing, bringing in the
   sheaves,
Bringing in the sheaves, bringing in the
   sheaves,
We shall come, rejoicing, bringing in the
   sheaves.

2 Sowing in the sunshine, sowing in the
   shadows,
Fearing neither clouds nor winter's
   chilling breeze;
By and by the harvest, and the labor
   ended,
We shall come, rejoicing, bringing in
   the sheaves.

3 Go, then, ever weeping, sowing for
   the master,
Tho' the loss sustain'd our spirit often
   grieves;
When our weeping's over, He will bid
   us welcome,
We shall come rejoicing, bringing in
   the sheaves.

171 Music, No. 5, Gems of Gospel Song.

1 I am dwelling on the mountain,
Where the golden sunlight gleams
O'er a land whose wondrous beauty
Far exceeds my fondest dreams;
Where the air is pure, ethereal,
Laden with the breath of flowers
That are blooming by the fountain,
'Neath the amaranthine bowers.

CHO.—Is not this the land of Beulah,.
Blessed, blessed land of light,
Where the flowers bloom forever,
And the sunlight fadeth not?

2 I can see far down the mountain,
Where I wandered weary years,
Often hindered in my journey
By the ghosts of doubts and fears,
Broken vows and disappointments
Thickly sprinkled all the way,
But the Spirit led unerring
To the land I hold to-day.

3 I am drinking at the fountain,
Where I ever would abide,
For I've tasted life's pure river,
And my soul is satisfied;
There's no thirsting for life's pleasures
Nor adorning, rich and gay,
For I've found a richer treasure,
One that fadeth not away.

172 Music, No. 216, Gems of Gospel Song.

1 Lord, I care not for riches,
Neither silver nor gold,
I would make sure of heaven,
I would enter the fold.
In the book of Thy kingdom,
With its pages so fair,
Tell me, Jesus, my Savior,
Is my name written there?

CHORUS.
Is my name written there,
On the page white and fair?
In the book of Thy kingdom,
Is my name written there?

2 Lord, my sins they are many,
Like the sands of the sea,
But thy blood, O my Savior!
Is sufficient for me;
For thy promise is written
In bright letters that glow,
"Though your sins be as scarlet,
I will make them like snow."

3 Oh! that beautiful city,
With its mansions of light,
With its glorified beings,
In pure garments of white,
Where no evil thing cometh,
To despoil what is fair;
Where the angels are watching,
Is my name written there?

173 Music, No. 191, Gems of Gospel Song.

1 I saw a happy pilgrim,
In shining garments clad,
And trav'ling up the mountain,
His countenance was glad;
He had no cares nor burdens,
He'd laid them at the cross,
The blood of Christ, his Savior,
Had wash'd him from all dross.

CHORUS.
Then palms of victory,
Crowns of glory,
Palms of victory,
We shall wear.

2 The summer sun was shining,
The sweat was on his brow;
His garments worn and dusty,
His step seemed very slow;
But he kept pressing onward,
For he was wending home,
Still shouting as he journeyed,
Deliverance will come.

3 I saw him in the evening,
The sun was bending low,
Had overtopped the mountain,
And reached the vale below;
He saw the golden city,
His everlasting home,
And shouted loud, Hosannah!
Deliverance will come.

174 Music, No. 159, Gems of Gospel Song.

1 Oh, blessed fellowship divine!
Oh, joy supremely sweet!
Companionship with Jesus here,
Makes life with bliss replete.
In union with the Purest One
I find my heav'n on earth begun.

CHORUS.
Oh, wondrous bliss, oh, joy sublime,
I've Jesus with me all the time,
Oh, wondrous bliss, oh, joy sublime,
I've Jesus with me all the time.

2 I'm walking close to Jesus' side,
So close 'hat I can hear
The softest whispers of his love,
In fellowship so dear.
And feel his great almighty hand
Protects me in this hostile land.

3 I'm leaning on his loving breast,
Along life's weary way;
My path, illumined by his smiles,
Grows brighter every day.
No foes, no woes, my heart can fear,
With my Almighty Friend so near.

175 Music, No. 21, Gems of Gospel Song.

1 Will you come, will you come,
With your poor broken heart,
Burden'd and sin-oppressed?
Lay it down at the feet
Of your Savior and Lord,
Jesus will give you rest.

CHORUS.
O happy rest, sweet, happy rest!
Jesus will give you rest.
Oh! why don't you come
In simple, trusting faith?
Jesus will give you rest.

2 Will you come, will you come?
There is mercy for you,
Balm for your aching breast;
Only come as you are,
And believe on his name,
Jesus will give you rest.

3 Will you come, will you come,
You have nothing to pay;
Jesus, who loves you best,
By his death on the cross,
Purchased life for your soul,
Jesus will give you rest.

176 Music, No. 16, Gems of Gospel Song.

1 Lord, I believe a rest remains
To all thy people known,
A rest where pure enjoyment reigns,
And thou art loved alone.

CHORUS.
I rest upon his promise, sure;
I come, I wait to prove
The cleansing of my heart from sin,
The fullness of His love.

2 A rest where all our soul's desire,
Is fix'd on things above;
Where fear, and sin and grief expire,
Cast out by perfect love.

3 Oh! that I now the rest might know,
Believe, and enter in;
Now, Saviour, now the power bestow,
And let me cease from sin.

177 Music, No. 45, Gems of Gospel Song.

How bright the hope that Calvary brings,
Where love divine with mercy blends;
How full the joy that all may find,
Where flows the blood can save and
cleanse.

CHORUS.
I am glad there is cleansing in the blood,
I am glad there is cleansing in the blood,
Tell the world, all the world,
There is cleansing in the Savior's blood.

'Tis there! 'tis there the soul may go,
And wash its sins and stains away;
Who gives up all,—who comes by faith,
This cleansing finds without delay.

178 Music, No. 63, Gems of Gospel Song.

I follow the footsteps of Jesus, my Lord,
His Spirit doth lead me along;
I walk in the path-way made plain by
His word,
And He fills all my soul with this song.

CHORUS.
Glory to God my spirit is free,
Glory to God, He purifies me! [be
I'm walking the highway, and joyful I'll
While following Jesus my Lord.

A leper he found me, polluted by sin,
From which he alone can set free;
He spake in His mercy, "I will, be thou
And He instantly purified me. [clean,"

A captive in woe to my prison of night
The Master hath opened the door;
Shout aloud of deliv'rance, ye angels of
light,
Praise His name, oh my soul, evermore.

179 Music, No. 66, Gems of Gospel Song.

1 Would you know why I love Jesus?
Why he is so dear to me?
'Tis because my blessed Jesus
From my sins has ransomed me.

CHORUS.
This is why I love my Jesus,
This is why I love him so,
He atoned for my transgressions,
He has washed me white as snow.

2 Would you know why I love Jesus?
Why he is so dear to me?
'Tis because the blood of Jesus
Fully saves and cleanses me.

3 Would you know why I love Jesus?
Why he is so dear to me?
'Tis because amid temptation,
He supports and strengthens me.

180 Music, No. 85, Gems of Gospel Song.

Why do you linger in darkness so long?
Jesus is waiting to save! [throng?
Have you not friends in the heavenly
Jesus is waiting to save!

CHORUS.
Come to him now, come to him now,
Jesus is waiting to save!
Come to him now, come to him now,
Jesus is waiting to save!

Time will not linger, how soon we must go!
Jesus is waiting to save!
Why turn away, and to Jesus say no?
Jesus is waiting to save!

Jesus is calling, "Oh, come unto me!"
Jesus is waiting to save!
Pardon is purchased, salvation is free;
Jesus is waiting to save!

181 Tune, By and By We Shall Meet Him.

1 The prize is set before us,
    To win, His words implore us,
  The eye of God is o'er us
    From on high ;
  His loving tones are calling
  While sin is dark, appalling,
  'Tis Jesus gently calling,
    He is nigh.

CHORUS.

By and by we shall meet Him,
By and by we shall meet Him,
And with Jesus reign in glory,
    By and by ;
By and by we shall meet Him,
By and by we shall meet Him,
And with Jesus reign in glory,
    By and by.

2 We'll follow where He leadeth,
  We'll pasture where He feedeth,
  We'll yield to Him who pleadeth
    From on high ;
  Then naught from Him shall sever,
  Our hope shall brighten ever,
  And faith shall fail us never,
    He is nigh.

182 Tune, Sweet By and By.

There's a land that is fairer than day,
  And by faith we can see it afar ;
For the Father waits over the way,
  To prepare us a dwelling place there.

CHORUS.

In the sweet by-and-by,
We shall meet on that beautiful shore,
  In the sweet by and by,
We shall meet on that beautiful shore.

We shall sing on that beautiful shore
  The melodious songs of the blest,
And our spirits shall sorrow no more,
  Not a sigh for the blessing of rest.

To our bountiful Father above
  We will offer our tribute of praise,
For the glorious gift of His love,
  And the blessings that hallow our days.

183 · Tune, Close to Thee.

1 Thou my everlasting portion,
    More than friend or life to me,
  All along my pilgrim journey,
    Saviour, let me walk with Thee.

CHORUS.

Close to Thee, close to Thee,
Close to Thee, close to Thee ;
All along my pilprim journey,
Saviour, let me walk with Thee.

2 Not for ease or worldly pleasure,
    Nor for fame my prayer shall be ;
  Gladly will I toil and suffer,
    Only let me walk with Thee.

184 Tune, Have You Been to Jesus ?

Have you been to Jesus for the cleansing
    power ?
Are you washed in the blood of the Lamb?
Are you fully trusting in his grace this
    hour ?
Are you washed in the blood of the Lamb?

CHORUS.

Are you washed in the blood,
In the soul-cleansing blood of the Lamb?
  Are your garments spotless ?
  Are they white as snow ?
Are you washed in the blood of the Lamb?

Are you walking daily by the Saviour's
    side ?
Are you washed in the blood of the Lamb?
Do you rest each moment in the Crucified?
Are you washed in the blood of the Lamb?

When the Bridegroom cometh, will your
    robes be white,
Pure and white in the blood of the Lamb?
Will your soul be ready for the mansions
    bright,
And be washed in the blood of the Lamb?

185 Tune, To the Rock Let Me Fly.

Oh, sometimes the shadows are deep,
  And rough seems the path to the goal,
And sorrows how often they sweep
  Like tempests down over the soul.

CHORUS.

Oh, then, to the Rock let me fly,
  To the Rock that is higher than I ;
Oh, then, to the Rock let me fly,
  To the Rock that is higher than I.

Oh, sometimes how long seems the day,
  And sometimes how heavy my feet ;
But toiling in life's dusty way,
  The Rock's blessed shadow, how sweet!

Oh, near to the Rock let me keep
  Or blessings, or sorrows prevail ;
Or climbing the mountain way steep,
  Or walking the shadowy vale.

186 Tune, Precious Name.

1 Take the name of Jesus with you,
    Child of sorrow and of woe—
  It will joy and comfort give you,
    Take it then where'er you go.

CHORUS.

Precious name, oh, how sweet !
Hope of earth and joy of heaven,
Precious name. oh, how sweet—
Hope of earth and joy of heaven.

2 Take the name of Jesus ever,
    As a shield from every snare ;
  If temptations 'round you gather,
    Breathe that holy name in prayer.

187

Dear Jesus I long to be perfectly whole,
I want Thee forever to live in my soul,
Break down every idol, cast out every foe,
Now wash me, and I shall be whiter
than snow.

CHORUS.

Whiter than snow, yes, whiter than snow,
Now wash me, and I shall be whiter than
snow.

Dear Jesus, for this I most humbly en- [treat,
I wait, blessed Lord, at Thy crucified feet,
By faith, for my cleansing, I see Thy
blood flow, [than snow.
Now wash me, and I shall be whiter

The blessing by faith I receive from
above, [love;
Oh, glory! my soul is made perfect in
My prayer has prevailed, and this mo-
ment I know, [snow.
The blood is applied, I am whiter than

188

He leadeth me! Oh! blessed thought,
Oh! words with heav'nly comfort fraught;
Whate'er I do, where'er I be,
Still 'tis God's hand that leadeth me.

CHORUS.

He leadeth me, He leadeth me;
By His own hand He leadeth me;
His faithful follower I would be,
For by His hand He leadeth me.

Sometimes 'mid scenes of deepest gloom,
Sometimes where Eden's bowers bloom;
By waters still o'er troubled sea—
Still 'tis his hand that leadeth me.

Lord, I would clasp thy hand in mine,
Nor ever murmur or repine,—
Content, whatever lot I see,
Since 'tis my God that leadeth me.

189

1 Behold a stranger at the door,
He gently knocks, has knock'd before;
Has waited long, is waiting still;
You treat no other friend so ill.

CHORUS.

O let the dear Saviour come in,
He'll cleanse thy heart from sin;
O keep him no more out at the door,
But let the dear Saviour come in.

2 O lovely attitude!—he stands
With melting heart and laded hands,
O matchless kindness!—and he shows
This matchless kindness to his foes.

3 But will he prove a friend indeed?
He will—the very friend you need;
The friend of sinners—yes, 'tis he,
With garments dyed on Calvary.

190

Lo! a voice is calling now, "Come away,
Come to Jesus and be saved while you
may;
He is waiting now your heart to receive,
If you only in his name will believe."

CHORUS.

"Yes, I will go,
To Jesus I will go and be saved."

All my sins, and follies too, I'll forsake,
And a vow to serve the Lord I will make;
All my wanderings from him I'll give o'er
And his follower will be evermore.

In his blessed word, I'll trust day by day,
Which reveals him as the Life, Truth,
and Way;
With the Holy Spirit's light as my guide,
From the narrow way I'll ne'er turn aside.

191

The cross, the cross, the blood-stained
cross,
The hallowed cross I see,
Reminding me of precious blood
That once was shed for me.

CHORUS.

Oh, the blood, the precious blood
That Jesus shed for me.
Upon the cross in crimson flood
Just now by faith I see.

The cross, the cross, the heavy cross,
The Saviour bore for me,
Which bowed Him to the earth with
grief,
On sad Mount Calvary.

How light! how light, this precious
cross,
Presented to my view;
And while with care I take it up,
Behold the crown my due.

192

1 I stand all bewildered with wonder,
And gaze on the ocean of love;
And over its waves to my spirit
Comes peace, like a heavenly dove.

CHORUS.

The cross now covers my sins,
The past is under the the blood,
I'm trusting in Jesus for all,
My will is the will of my God.

2 I struggled and wrestled to win it,
The blessing that setteth me free;
But when I had ceased from my struggle
His peace Jesus gave unto me.

3 He laid his hand on me, and heal'd me,
And bade me be every whit whole;
I touched but the hem of his garment,
And glory came thrilling my soul.

193   Tune, Alone With Jesus.

1 O who'll stand up for Jesus,
   The lowly Nazarine ?
And raise the blood-stained banner
   Amid the hosts of sin ?

CHORUS.

The cross for Christ I'll cherish,
   Its crucifixion bear ;
All hail, reproach and sorrow,
   If Jesus leads me there.

2 O who will follow Jesus
   Amid reproach and shame ?
Where others shrink and falter,
   Who'll glory in his name ?

3 My all to Christ I've given,
   My talents, time and voice,
Myself, my reputation ;
   The lone way is my choice.

194   Tune, Gate Open Wide.

1 There is a gate stands open wide,
   And through its portals gleaming,
A radiance from the cross afar,
   The Savior's love revealing.

CHORUS.

Oh! depth of mercy, can it be,
   That gate stands open wide for me,
Stands open wide, both night and day,
   Stands open wide for me ?

2 That gate stands open wide for all,
   Who seek through it salvation ;
The rich and poor, the great and small
   Of every tribe and nation.

3 Press onward then, though foes may
    frown,
   While mercy's gate is open ;
Accept the cross and win the crown,
   Love's everlasting token.

195   Tune, Keep Me Near the Cross.

1 Jesus keep me near the cross,
   There's a precious fountain,
Free to all—a healing stream,
   Flows from Calvary's mountain.

CHORUS.

In the cross, in the cross,
   Be my glory ever,
Till my raptured soul shall find
   Rest beyond the river.

2 Near the cross, a trembling soul,
   Love and mercy found me ;
There the bright and morning-star
   Shed its beams around me.

3 Near the Cross! O Lamb of God,
   Bring its scenes before me,
Help me walk from day to day
   With its shadows o'er me.

196   Tune, Pass Me Not.

1 Pass me not, O gentle Savior,
   Hear my humble cry ;
While on others thou art smiling,
   Do not pass me by,

CHORUS.

Savior, Savior,
   Hear my humble cry,
While on others thou art calling,
   Do not pass me by.

2 Trusting only in thy merit,
   Would I seek thy face ;
Heal my wounded, broken spirit,
   Save me by thy grace.

3 Thou the spring of all my comfort,
   More than life to me,
Whom have I on earth beside thee ?
   Whom in heaven but thee ?

197   Tune, I Am Coming, Lord.

1 I hear thy welcome voice
   That calls me, Lord, to thee,
For cleansing in thy precious blood
   That flowed on Calvary.

CHORUS.

I am coming, Lord !
   Coming now to thee !
Wash me, cleanse me in the blood
   That flowed on Calvary.

2 Tho' coming weak and vile,
   Thou dost my strength assure ;
Thou dost my vileness fully cleanse,
   Till spotless all and pure.

2 'Tis Jesus calls me on
   To perfect faith and love ;
To perfect hope, and peace, and trust,
   For earth and heaven above.

198   Tune, Beulah Land.

I've reach'd the land of corn and wine,
And all its riches freely mine ;
Here shines undimm'd one blissful day,
For all my night has passed away.

CHORUS.

O Beulah land, sweet Beulah land,
As on thy highest mount I stand,
I look away across the sea,
Where mansions are prepared for me,
And view the shining glory shore,
My heav'n, my home for evermore.

The Savior comes and walks with me,
And sweet communion here have we ;
He gently leads me with his hand,
For this is heaven's border land.

A sweet perfume upon the breeze
Is borne from ever vernal trees,
And flow'rs that never fading grow
Where streams of life forever flow.

INDEX OF TITLES.

	NO.		NO.
A child of the King	43	Mighty to save	41
At the cross	81	'Neath the shadow of His wing	68
Be guiding me	137	Our cherished loved ones	28
Beautiful Home	55	Prayer for guidance	33
Bless the Lord	2	Peace divine	62
Church of God awake	58	Prodigal child come home	22
Clinging to the cross	51	Perfect peace	93
Calvary	64	Resting	5
Cleansing Balm	66	Redeemed	65
Church rallying song	78	Rejoicing evermore	79
Come and help us	85	Roll the stone away	87
Cast thy burden on the Lord	77	Ring, ring the bells	89
Depth of mercy	121	Redeeming Love	27
Don't be too late	70	Suffer the children to come	105
Follow thou me	135	Simply trusting	133
Fill me now	115	Satisfied	122
For you and for me	82	Silent night	114
Full salvation	48	Saved by grace alone	73
Go forth men of God	18	Stay, sinner, stay	67
God is coming	38	Sing of my Redeemer	50
Glory to Christ my King	84	Saved to the uttermost	53
Glorious fountain	142	Seek ye the kingdom of God	46
Give me peace	109	Sweetly resting	45
Glory to His name	126	Shout for joy	42
He is mine	141	Stand the storm	19
Homeward bound	140	Sing of His love	12
He will gather the wheat	49	Since I have been redeemed	20
He knows	97	The harvest is passing	8
Hear Him calling	80	Touch not, taste not, handle not	9
He is coming	74	There is room	11
Have you the garments of white	54	The wandering stranger	14
Heavenly Shepherd	40	The altered motto	15
He ransomed me	7	Tell it out	24
He would not go away	61	Treasures of heaven	30
I've washed my robes	6	There is joy in heaven	31
I will follow	10	The cross is all my glory	47
I come just as I am	23	There is life in a look	75
I'll be there	37	Take my hand, dear Jesus	101
I will give you rest	72	To-morrow it may be too late	83
I will trust	91	The ten Virgins	116
I am Jesus' little lamb	104	They come	124
I'll live for Him	127	The half has never yet been told	128
Jesus lead the way	113	Unity	130
Jesus is mine	111	Up for Jesus stand	17
Jesus is calling	107	When we arrive at home	4
Jesus saves me all the time	103	Weary one rest	26
Just waiting	69	What did Jesus say	29
Lord abide with me	35	We mean this world for God	35
Let Him in	39	Will it pay	36
Looking into Jesus	44	What a wonderful Savior	138
Lilly of the valley	56	Will you stand	52
Lead me safely on	86	Weighed in the balance	59
Look to Jesus	108	Who shall be able?	60
Living waters flow	76	We shall sing	63
My dream	117	Waiting	95
Mary Magdalen	57	We'll press this battle on	98
My angel mother	32	We will have a happy time	134
My boy is coming home	21	Whiter than the snow	16

Index of Familiar Hymns.

Alas! and did my Savior bleed 118
A charge to keep I have........... 98
Arise, my soul arise 155
All hail the power of Jesus' name... 150
Are you weary, are you heavy laden? 161
At the sounding of the trumpet...... 167
Are you ready for the Bridegroom? 168
Am I a soldier of the cross?.......... 99

Blessed assurance, Jesus is mine.... 94
Blest be the tie that binds.............. 152
Behold a stranger at the door!........ 189
Blow ye, the trumpet blow............. 143

Children of the heavenly King....... 88
Come thou fount of every blessing... 123
Come ye sinners, poor and needy.... 162
Come ye that love the Lord............ 90

Down at the cross........................ 126
Depth of mercy........................... 121
Dear Jesus, I long to be perfectly
wnole 187

Forever here my rest shall be........ 91

Grace, 'tis a charming sound........ 73

Hark! the voice of Jesus calling.... 144
His name yields the richest perfume. 106
How bright the hope that Calvary
brings!.............. 177
Have you been to Jesus for the clean-
ing power?....................... 184
He leadeth me, Oh, blessed thought! 188

I am coming to the cross.............. 160
I will follow thee, my Savior.......... 165
I have found repose for my weary
soul....................... ... 169
I am dwelling on the mountain...... 171
I saw a happy pilgrim 173
I follow the footsteps of Jesus, my
Lord................................. 178
I stand all bewildered with wonder.. 192
I hear thy welcome voice............. 197
I've reached the land of corn and
wine 198
I love thy Church, O God.............. 112

Jesus, keep me near the cross........ 195
Just as I am......... 153
Jesus, I my cross have taken......... 145
Jesus my all, to heaven is gone 37
Jesus, lover of my soul................. 120

Look to Jesus 108
Love divine, all love excelling........ 154
Lord, I care not for riches............. 172

Lord, I believe a rest remains......... 176
Lo, a voice is calling now, come away. 190
Long have I striven from sin to flee. 125

My Jesus I love thee................... 100
My life flows on in endless song...... 147
My body, soul and spirit............... 157
My Jesus I love thee.................... 100

Nearer, my God, to Thee... 111
Now crucified with Christ I am...... 166

Oh, for a thousand tongues to sing! 3
Oh, for a heart to praise my God!... 110
Oh, think of the home over there!... 102
O happy day that fixed my choice!.. 119
Oh, now I see the crimson wave!.... 136
Oh, blessed fellowship divine!......... 174
Oh, who'll stand up for Jesus?....... 193
Oh, sometimes the shadows are deep. 185

Pass me not, O gentle Savior......... 196
Plunged in a gulf of dark despair!... 129
Precious promise, God hath given... 92

Rock of ages, cleft for me 158

Sowing in the morning.................. 170
Stand up, stand up for Jesus.......... 148
Show pity Lord, O Lord forgive...... 149
Savior, more than life to me.......... 159

There is a gate stands open wide.... 194
The cross, the cross, the blood-stained
cross.................. 191
Take the name of Jesus with you... 186
Thou, my everlasting portion........ 183
There's a land that is fairer than day. 182
The prize is set before us.............. 181
Take my life, and let it be............ 163
There is a fountain filled with blood. 142
Tho' troubles assail, and dangers
affright................... 79
There is a land of pure delight....... 70

When I survey the wondrous cross. 7
What a friend we have in Jesus!..... 96
We're a band that shall conquer the
foe............ 131
We will hope, we will trust in the
Lord................ 132
When I can read my title clear 151
We are out on the ocean sailing...... 156
What poor despised company........ 164
Will you come, will you come?....... 175
Would you know why I love Jesus?.. 179
Why do you linger in darkness so
long? 180

Zion stands with hills surrounded... 146

www.ingramcontent.com/pod-product-compliance
Lightning Source LLC
Chambersburg PA
CBHW030615270326
41927CB00007B/1191